Judging
on a
Collegial
Court

Constitutionalism and Democracy

GREGG IVERS AND
KEVIN T. MCGUIRE,
EDITORS

Judging on a Collegial Court

INFLUENCES ON FEDERAL APPELLATE DECISION MAKING

Virginia A. Hettinger, Stefanie A. Lindquist, and Wendy L. Martinek

UNIVERSITY OF VIRGINIA PRESS   CHARLOTTESVILLE AND LONDON

University of Virginia Press
© 2006 by the Rector and Visitors of the University of Virginia
All rights reserved
Printed in the United States of America on acid-free paper

First published 2006

First paperback edition published 2007
ISBN 978-0-8139-2697-1 (paper)

9 8 7 6 5 4 3 2 1

The Library of Congress has cataloged the hardcover edition as follows:

LIBRARY OF CONGRESS CATALOGING-IN-PUBLICATION DATA

Hettinger, Virginia A., 1961–
   Judging on a collegial court : influences on federal appellate decision making /
Virginia A. Hettinger, Stefanie A. Lindquist, and Wendy L. Martinek.
      p.   cm. — (Constitutionalism and democracy)
   Includes bibliographical references and index.
   ISBN 0-8139-2518-5 (cloth : alk. paper)
   1. Judicial process—United States. 2. Judicial opinions—United States. 3. Dissent-
ing opinions—United States. 4. Appellate courts—United States. I. Lindquist,
Stefanie A., 1963– II. Martinek, Wendy L. III. Title. IV. Series.
KF8750.H48 2006
347.73′24—dc22

                                                                                     2005016954

For Harold
from all of us

For Vin
V.A.H.

For Rudy
S.A.L.

For Judith A. Martinek
and Richard J. Martinek
W.L.M.

CONTENTS

TABLES

ACKNOWLEDG-MENTS

Everyone values collegial relationships. We were fortunate enough to forge many such relationships as we labored on this book and related work. Not the least of these is the relationship we have developed with one another. Others should be so fortunate to find coauthors who bring out the best, both personally and professionally, in one another.

We were also quite fortunate to benefit from an array of other individuals. First among them is Harold J. Spaeth, to whom we dedicate our book. His careful reading of the manuscript and unflagging encouragement of our collaboration and efforts buoyed us on hard days and helped us push through to completion. We are grateful to him for his unwavering support. He is a mentor par excellence.

In addition, we would like to thank the editors, Kevin McGuire and Gregg Ivers, for assisting us in refining the manuscript, the anonymous reviewers for their helpful suggestions, and Dick Holway of the University of Virginia Press for his enthusiasm for the manuscript and careful shepherding of the manuscript (and us!) through the publication process. We also thank the U.S. Administrative Office of the Courts for use of a figure from their Web site.

Though all of the work contained herein is original to this book, some of our earlier work gave rise to our idea for this book. In particular, chapter 3 is a much-modified version of "Separate Opinion Writing on the United States Courts of Appeals" (Hettinger, Lindquist, and Martinek 2003c), which appeared in *American Politics Quarterly.* Chapter 4 extends the work that we first presented at the 2002 annual meeting of the Midwest Political Science Association in Chicago, Illinois, and which appeared in "Comparing Attitudinal and Strategic Accounts of Dissenting Behavior on the U.S. Courts of Appeals" (Hettinger, Lindquist, and Martinek 2004), published in the *American Journal of Political Science*. And chapter 5 was inspired, in part, by a paper we presented at the 2002 annual meeting of the American Political Science Association in Boston, Massachusetts, and which later appeared in "The Role and Impact of Chief Judges on the United States Courts of Appeals" (Hettinger, Lindquist, and Martinek 2003b) in the *Justice System Journal*.

We were fortunate to have many individuals comment on and respond to various stages of this work, and we wish to thank them all, including Carl Baar, Vanessa Baird, Sara C. Benesh, Samuel J. Best, David H. Clark, Paul M. Collins Jr., Martha Ginn, Sheldon Goldman, Susan Haire, Roger Hartley, Thomas L. Holbrook, Richard Pacelle, Rorie Spill, Susette Talarico, Steven R. Van Winkle, Paul J. Wahlbeck, and Stephen L. Wasby. We also wish to thank Sesselja Arnadotir, Paul M. Collins Jr., and Zhaoying Du for their able research assistance.

Hettinger wishes to thank the Department of Political Science at the University of Connecticut for providing a course reduction, graduate research assistants, and a working environment that is supportive and enjoyable. She also thanks Micheal Giles, Thomas Walker, and Christopher Zorn for nurturing her interest in judicial politics. Finally, members of the Hettinger, Walker, and Moscardelli families have supported her in their own special ways, and for that she is especially grateful.

Lindquist would like to thank John Murphy, Susette Talarico, and Susan Haire for their support during the writing of this book, as well as her mother, Nancy Lou, whose intellectual energy and remarkable character is, and has always been, truly inspiring.

Martinek is especially grateful to Harold J. Spaeth, not only for his guidance on this project, but also for his steadfast mentoring over the past eight years. Martinek further gratefully acknowledges the support of Jean-Pierre Mileur, Dean of Harpur College at Binghamton University, for a Dean's Research Semester Award, which gave her valuable time to work on this book. Martinek also acknowledges her very fine colleagues in the Department of Political Science at Binghamton University, who make coming to work such a delight. Finding a group of smarter, more intellectually engaged, and funnier individuals it is hard to imagine.

As in all our previous collaborative work, our names are presented alphabetically; equal contributions were made by each.

Judging
on a
Collegial
Court

Introduction

Cass Sunstein begins his book, *Why Societies Need Dissent,* with a quote from Hans Christian Anderson's story "The Emperor's New Clothes": "A child, however, who had no important job and could only see things as his eyes showed them to him, went up to the carriage, 'The Emperor is naked,' he said" (Sunstein 2003, 1). Unlike those self-interested citizens who persisted in acquiescing to the emperor's deception, the child, unencumbered by social or economic pressures, saw reality clearly and thus registered his disbelief. The moral to the fable, of course, is that social pressure to conform may cause collective blindness. As Sunstein notes, collective blindness has many far-reaching consequences, such as in the areas of corporate governance (witness Enron, for example) or international relations (the Bay of Pigs disaster). As a means to remedy the "new-clothes" mentality, the willingness to dissent is salubrious because it serves to check group tendencies to converge on nonoptimal solutions.

Within appellate courts, however, collective action by collegial panels is *intended* to promote optimal decision making. On appeal, litigants can be assured of review by a body composed of several judges. The rationale underlying this system is that arbitrary decision making in collegial bodies will be reduced by the moderating influence of alternative points of view. Since the panel outcome is governed by majority rule, the litigant will not be subjected to the errant or unconventional ideas of any one panel member. And because the rule of law *depends* on the consistency born of such conventionalism, the appeals process helps ensure that legal norms will not vary in their application solely on the basis of an appellate panel's composition.

Yet Sunstein demonstrates that this legal consistency may be undermined when the composition of an appellate panel accentuates like views (generating what he refers to as "ideological amplification"). When judges are sitting exclusively with like-minded colleagues, they tend to render decisions that are ideologically consistent with the group's collective preferences. This "group polarization" phenomenon arises, in part, because *no threat of dissent exists* that might otherwise call the panel's decision to the attention of superior courts (Cross and Tiller 1998). Not all agree, however, that dissents represent an unmitigated good. While some see them as critical to the long-term development of the law, others do not. Some critics view dissents as evidence of an irresponsible and fractious decision-making process. Dissents have the potential to compromise the clarity of the law and thereby serve as a source of additional confusion in an already-complicated legal world. In the U.S. Courts of Appeals, judges file dissents in a minority of their decisions; concurrences are even less frequent. Yet, on occasion the threat of dissent does materialize into an actual dissent. Regardless of the normative debates that rage on regarding the value of dissent, the determinants of separate opinion writing should be of central scholarly interest.

In this book, to answer the simple question of whether judges are more or less likely to dissent or concur in particular circumstances, we undertake an analysis of separate-opinion writing in the federal appeals courts. In answering that question, we hope to shed light on judges' calculations regarding the choice to deviate from consensus-oriented behavior, something we refer to as horizontal dissensus. This inquiry is critical, because, by refusing to conform to the panel majority, judges who file separate opinions either maintain the integrity of the federal judiciary or undermine its legitimacy, depending on one's point of view.

A dissent is not the only form of judicial behavior that has consequences regarding the optimality of decision making. While they are subject to the potentially arbitrary behavior of a single judge at the trial level, unsatisfied litigants are not without recourse. The appellate process affords them at least some safeguard against capricious behavior by trial court judges. Appellate review of a trial court ruling not only serves to ameliorate the consequences of an errant lower court ruling for an individual litigant, but it also serves a further, broader, purpose. Reversal, whether actualized or not, can serve as a tool to foster (though, of course, not necessarily guarantee) stability in the legal system. From this perspective, in the absence of review by an appellate body—with the attendant potential for reversal—it is difficult for others (litigants, attorneys, judges, policy-makers) to have much confidence in the consistency of legal rulings, which collectively create policy, because there is no mechanism for correction.

As with dissents, however, not all perspectives on reversals are equally sanguine. Some legal observers and scholars see reversals as creating confusion by producing different winners at different levels of the judiciary. Regardless of one's normative position, reversals—like dissents—are a fact of legal life. In fact, in the U.S. Courts of Appeals, reversals are more common than dissents. And, like dissents, reversals play an important role in the development of the law, if for no other reason than they serve to assure consistency in the application of the law.

In light of their importance, we also undertake an analysis of reversals of U.S. District Court rulings by the U.S. Courts of Appeals. Here, we hope to shed light on judges' calculations regarding the choice to upset an existing legal outcome, what we have termed vertical dissensus. Understanding the dynamic that gives rise to such dissensus is essential if we are to understand how the appellate process shapes the content and the consistency of the law.

We undertake our analyses of horizontal and vertical dissensus by focusing on the behavioral aspects of disagreement within a panel and between the levels of the federal judicial hierarchy. We predicate our analyses of these phenomena on the fundamental tenet of the behavioral tradition: individual attitudes or preferences play a role in judicial decision making. Our findings with regard to horizontal dissensus comport with that fundamental tenet. Our findings with regard to vertical dissensus, however, do not, at least not in a direct sense. Recognizing that explanations of behavior appropriately include factors other than individual attitudes, we also consider strategic, institutional, and legal explanations as well. Using such an integrated approach is appropriate for two reasons. First, it is consistent with the development of scholarly inquiry in studies of judicial behavior. Second, it is especially appropriate given the unique position occupied by the U.S. Courts of Appeals in the judicial hierarchy. This integrated approach allows us to recognize the constraints and freedoms that judges and panels on the courts of appeals may experience. In doing this, we hope that this book contributes to the body of empirical literature that adds to our understanding of judicial behavior.

We also hope that this book fits within a larger scholarly tradition of studying appellate courts using social scientific techniques and comprehensive databases. In a recent book, for example, Donald Songer, Reginald Sheehan, and Susan Haire (2000) used the U.S. Court of Appeals Database funded by the National Science Foundation (NSF) to explore longitudinal trends in decision making on those courts. The large-sample database, encompassing the years 1925–88, enabled the authors to explore the circuit courts' agendas, litigant participation, staffing, and ideological case outcomes over time, thus providing the first longitudinal portrait of the federal appellate judiciary and its decisional outputs. Jeffrey Segal and Harold Spaeth (1993, 2002) rely on the NSF-funded U.S. Supreme Court Database to explore the determinants of Supreme Court justices' votes on the merits, as did Brenner and Spaeth (1995). Without these comprehensive databases, research of this depth and breadth could not be conducted.

This book is intended to follow in this vein of research. Specifically, we rely on the U.S. Court of Appeals Database to build on the work already conducted by Songer, Sheehan, and Haire (2000) by exploring the decision-making dynamics on individual circuit panels, with particular attention to judges' choices to write separate opinions, whether concurring or dissenting, and panel decisions to reverse the district court. Although most of the decisions on the U.S. Courts of Appeals are unanimous, an important minority of those decisions represents situations in which judges breach the consensus norm to register their disagreement with the panel majority. These rare instances of disagreement represent significant events warranting in-depth analysis of the circumstances under which they develop. Lower court reversal is a more common phenomenon, and it, too, represents an action with significant import, import that makes unraveling the dynamic that gives rise to it important.

The following research is therefore not only situated within the tradition of longitudinal work by Songer et al., but also by those scholars such as Sheldon Goldman, who have demonstrated a keen interest in explaining and predicting dissensus on appellate courts (e.g., Goldman, 1966, 1975). We hope to assist readers in understanding the critical contextual and interpersonal nature of such dissensus—of both the horizontal and vertical kind—within these august legal institutions.

ONE

Horizontal and Vertical Dissensus

In this chapter, we explore two forms of dissensus. The first is horizontal dissensus, or that which occurs within a three-judge panel on the courts of appeals. Judges signal this form of dissensus by writing separate opinions that take the form of a dissent or a concurrence. The second is vertical dissensus, which occurs when a court of appeals panel disagrees with the lower court over the proper resolution of the case. This form of dissensus is observed when the court of appeals reverses the lower court's decision, either in whole or in part.

Juan Ramirez-Lopez and the Power of Dissent

In the spring of 2000, Juan Ramirez-Lopez and fifteen other illegal immigrants from Mexico crossed into the United States through the mountains of San Diego County. Unfortunately for the travelers, the weather was exceptionally cold in the mountains and one of the immigrants died of hypothermia. On March 6 Ramirez-Lopez and the remaining fourteen immigrants were arrested and Ramirez-Lopez was hospitalized for frostbite. Soon thereafter, border patrol agents interviewed Ramirez-Lopez, who waived his Miranda rights as well as his right to retain otherwise deportable witnesses. He also denied being the leader of the party.

When the other fourteen members of the group were interviewed, two claimed that Ramirez-Lopez was leading the group from Mexico, but twelve others denied that he was the guide, claiming that their guide had abandoned them or that they never had a guide. Nine of these twelve witnesses were then immediately deported to Mexico. Meanwhile, Ramirez-Lopez was charged with and tried for smuggling aliens and with the act of transporting aliens resulting in death. A key element of the charges involved whether Ramirez-Lopez was, in fact, leading the group from Mexico. The deportation of nine members of the party meant that Ramirez-Lopez was deprived of their testimony at trial, testimony that would have exonerated him as group leader. In addition, although the border patrol agents took careful and detailed notes on the witnesses' statements, those notes were inadmissible under rules limiting hearsay testimony. Ramirez-Lopez was subsequently convicted.

On appeal to the U.S. Court of Appeals for the Ninth Circuit, Ramirez-Lopez challenged his conviction on the grounds that (1) the district court judge had erred in failing to admit the exculpatory statements and notes recorded by the border patrol agents, (2) the deportation of witnesses whose testimony would have supported his defense violated his due process rights, and (3) a two-day delay in the arraignment violated his rights to a speedy trial. In *United States v. Ramirez-Lopez,*[1] the Ninth Circuit panel affirmed his conviction over the dissent of Judge Alex Kozinski. According to the majority of the three-judge appellate court panel, the defendant's rights had not been violated nor had the trial judge made any errors concerning the admissibility of evidence.

In response to the majority opinion upholding Ramirez-Lopez's conviction, Judge Kozinski's dissenting opinion begins with the following imaginary dialogue between the defendant and his lawyer:

LAWYER: Juan, I have good news and bad news.

RAMIREZ-LOPEZ: OK, I'm ready. Give me the bad news first.

LAWYER: The bad news is that the Ninth Circuit affirmed your conviction and you're going to spend many years in federal prison.

RAMIREZ-LOPEZ: Oh, man, that's terrible. I'm so disappointed. But you said there's good news too, right?

LAWYER: Yes, excellent news! I'm very excited.

RAMIREZ-LOPEZ: OK, I'm ready for some good news, let me have it.

LAWYER: Well, here it goes: You'll be happy to know that you had a perfect trial. They got you fair and square!

RAMIREZ-LOPEZ: How can that be? Didn't they keep me in jail for two days without letting me see a judge or a lawyer? Weren't they supposed to take me before a judge right away?

LAWYER: Yes, they sure were. But it's OK because you didn't show that it harmed you. We have a saying here in America: No harm, no foul.

Judge Kozinski then focuses the dialogue on the exculpatory hearsay evidence in the agents' notes:

RAMIREZ-LOPEZ: What do you mean no harm? There were twelve guys in my party who said I wasn't the guide, and they sent nine of them back to Mexico.

LAWYER: Yeah, but so what? Seeing the judge sooner wouldn't have helped you.

RAMIREZ-LOPEZ: The judge could have given me a lawyer and my lawyer could have talked to those guys before the Migra sent them back.

LAWYER: What difference would that have made?

RAMIREZ-LOPEZ: My lawyer could have taken notes, figured out which guys to keep here and which ones to send back.

LAWYER: Hey, not to worry, dude. The government did it all for you. They talked to everyone, they took notes and they kept the witnesses that would best help your case. Making sure you had a fair trial was their number one priority.

RAMIREZ-LOPEZ: No kidding, man. They did all that for me?

LAWYER: They sure did. Is this a great country or what?

RAMIREZ-LOPEZ: OK, I see it now, but there's one thing that still confuses me.

LAWYER: What's that, Juan?

RAMIREZ-LOPEZ: You see, the government took all those great notes to help me, just so we'd know what all those guys said.

LAWYER: Right, I saw them, and they were very good notes. Clear, specific, detailed. Good grammar and syntax. All told, I'd say those were some great notes.

RAMIREZ-LOPEZ: And twelve of those guys all said I wasn't the guide.

LAWYER: Absolutely! Our government never hides the ball. The government of Iraq or Afghanistan or one of those places might do this, but not ours. If twelve guys said you weren't the guide, everybody knows about it.

RAMIREZ-LOPEZ: Except the jury. I was there at the trial, and I remember the jury never saw the notes. And the officers who testified never told the jury that twelve of the fourteen guys that were with me said I wasn't the guide.

LAWYER: Right. . . .

RAMIREZ-LOPEZ: The jury was supposed to decide whether I was the guide or not, right? Don't you think they might have had a reasonable doubt if they'd heard that twelve of the fourteen guys in my party said it wasn't me?

LAWYER: He-he-he! You'd think that only if you didn't go to law school. Lawyers and judges know better. . . .

The imaginary conversation then turns to the significance of the rules excluding hearsay and how, in Ramirez-Lopez's case, the exclusion of the hearsay evidence deprived the jury of critical evidence:

RAMIREZ-LOPEZ: I see what you mean. But how about the notes? Surely the jury would have gotten a different picture if they had just seen the notes of nine guys saying I wasn't the guide. That wouldn't have taken too long.

LAWYER: Wrong again, Juan! Those notes were hearsay and in this country we don't admit hearsay.

RAMIREZ-LOPEZ: How come?

LAWYER: The guys writing down what the witnesses said could have made a mistake.

RAMIREZ-LOPEZ: You mean, like maybe one of those twelve guys said, "Juan *was* the guide," and the guy from Immigration made a mistake and wrote down, "Juan *was not* the guide"?

LAWYER: Exactly.

RAMIREZ-LOPEZ: You're right again, it probably happened just that way. I bet those guys from Immigration wrote down, "Juan wasn't the guide," even when the witnesses said loud and clear I was the guide—just to be extra fair to me.

LAWYER: Absolutely, that's the kind of guys they are.

RAMIREZ-LOPEZ: You're very lucky to be working with guys like that.

LAWYER: Amen to that. I thank my lucky stars every Sunday in church.

Judge Kozinski's tongue-in-cheek approach was effective. Following publication of the dissent, the government dismissed the charges against Ramirez-Lopez, released him from prison, and sent him back to Mexico. Yet Judge Kozinski's dissent did not identify any serious flaws in the trial court's legal reasoning or in the law as applied on appeal. Instead, Kozinski demonstrated that even the clear application of legal rules may yield an unjust result (Fisher 2003). The government apparently agreed.

Judge Kozinski's dissent in *Ramirez-Lopez* unmistakably demonstrates the potentially powerful impact of a separate appellate opinion. A dissent like Judge Kozinski's illustrates the continual conflict in the legal system over the definition of our shared principles or values. For this reason, scholars have demonstrated a keen interest in understanding why appellate judges choose to file a separate opinion and thus opt to engage in this act of "civil disobedience" against the majority. In this book, we follow in this scholarly tradition by evaluating the determinants of separate opinions to provide a clearer picture of when and why judges choose to exercise their prerogative to deviate from the majority's conclusions or opinion. In other words, we seek to understand the dynamics of dissensus among judges on the courts of appeals. Since such dissensus involves judges on the same court, we have labeled it "horizontal dissensus."

Horizontal dissensus is not the only important form of dissensus we observe. While a dissent represents disagreement among judges operating at the same level of the judicial hierarchy, appellate court reversal of a lower court represents a form of disagreement among judges on different levels within that hierarchy and, as such, can be thought of as "vertical dissensus." When a circuit panel reverses a district court ruling, it is a formal and official declaration of such a disagreement between superior and subordinate judges in the federal judicial system. Like dissents, the disagreement embodied in the reversal of a lower court uncovers the struggle over the content of our social compact, a struggle inherent in our legal system. The evidence suggests, however, that appeals court judges do not generally relish the notion of entering the fray and puncturing collegial relations between the circuit and district courts, as the case of *Reid-Walen v. Hansen* illustrates.[2]

A Jamaica Vacation Gone Awry

Jayne Reid-Walen and her husband, Gary Walen, had vacationed before in Jamaica and decided to make Jamaica their vacation destination yet again. As they had in the past, the Walens opted to stay at the Yellowbird Sea-Tel, located on Seven Mile Beach in Negril, Jamaica. Run by Leroy and Irene Hansen, the Yellowbird Sea-Tel consists of a cluster of cottages and motel rooms run as a small bed and breakfast. Guests of the Yellowbird have access to the establishment's extensive grounds, which include a swimming area adjacent to the beach on which the Yellowbird sits. While swimming in this area, Reid-Walen was struck and seriously injured by a motorboat operated by a man who was offering boat rides to guests of the Yellowbird, though he himself was not associated with the Yellowbird Sea-Tel in any way.

Reid-Walen's injuries required hospitalization in Florida, and she and her husband sought damages from the Hansens for those injuries, arguing that the Hansens were negligent in failing to take reasonable steps to exclude motorboats from the designated swimming area. Before the merits of Reid-Walen's tort suit were ever considered, however, legal wrangling ensued over the appropriate venue for the case. The Walens first brought suit in the U.S. District Court for the Southern District of Florida in the Eleventh Circuit. For their part, the Hansens immediately sought the dismissal of the case based on the argument that it had not been filed in the appropriate court. Declining to dismiss the suit, the Florida district court instead transferred the case to the U.S. District Court for the Eastern District of Missouri, located in the Eighth Circuit, because that is where the Hansens resided when they were not otherwise living in Jamaica. The Hansens again sought to have the suit dismissed, also for reasons related to venue. This time, however, they argued that the suit should be dismissed based on the legal doctrine of *forum non conveniens.* Literally translated from Latin as inconvenient forum, the doctrine of *forum non conveniens* permits a court either to transfer a case or to decline to hear it altogether if the location of that court is inconvenient for the litigants or the witnesses. Of course, judges have not interpreted this doctrine to apply in the case of just any sort of inconvenience. All lawsuits, private or public, entail some inconvenience for the parties involved, who must appear in court at locations that may not be at all convenient and often interrupting lives that are already otherwise crowded with work and family commitments.

In this particular case, Judge George Gunn Jr. of the U.S. District Court for the Eastern District of Missouri had to decide if his court would be *forum non conveniens,* as the Hansens argued. It was an unusual argument in that the Hansens were asserting that a court located in the United States, in the state in which they resided, was less convenient than one located in a foreign country. But, as the Hansens further argued, understanding what happened on the day that Reid-Walen suffered her terrible injuries would require on-site examination of the location as well as testimony from key witnesses who resided in Jamaica. When the Hansens' arguments proved persuasive to Judge Gunn and the suit was dismissed, the Walens were not ready simply to accept Judge Gunn's decision as final. Instead, they filed an appeal with the U.S. Court of Appeals for the Eighth Circuit. There the case was heard by a panel consisting of Court of Appeals judges Donald Lay, Gerald Heaney, and William H. Timbers. Writing the majority opinion, which was joined by Judge Heaney, Chief Judge Lay reversed Judge Gunn's decision dismissing the suit. The majority then remanded the suit to the lower court for further proceedings. In doing so, Chief Judge Lay was careful to say, "Of course, we reverse the district court with great reluctance . . . ."[3] The majority opinion certainly did not include harsh language that could be construed as evidence of disdain for Judge Gunn's legal acumen or expertise in general.

Nonetheless, Judge Timbers was not happy with the ruling of his colleagues. Indeed, Judge Timbers was so unhappy that he drafted a rather lengthy dissenting opinion, chastising the majority as having crafted a "creative argument" to arrive at its result. Judge Timbers made clear that he felt "the majority merely substitute[d] its opinion for that of the district court."[4] Simply put, Judge Timbers felt the majority had not shown the appropriate deference to the district judge's judgment and had, thereby, usurped the district judge's role. In short, Judge Timbers was displeased with the reversal of the lower court and expressed his displeasure with that display of vertical dissensus by engaging in his own display of horizontal dissensus.

What the *Ramirez-Lopez* and *Reid-Walen* cases illustrate is that both separate opinions and lower court reversal represent conflicts of values, conflicts that have the power to influence both outcomes in individual cases and the shape of the law's development. They also implicate norms of behavior regarding collegial relations, both among circuit court judges and between circuit court and district court judges. These value conflicts and their expression are not trivial matters. They are meaningful not only for the litigants in particular cases but also for how the federal judiciary operates. Their importance in these regards demands rigorous scrutiny, scrutiny we undertake in this book.

The U.S. Courts of Appeals in the Federal Judicial System

The analyses of horizontal and vertical dissensus we conduct in later chapters of this book draw on data from the U.S. Courts of Appeals (Songer 2002), the major intermediate appellate courts in the federal system. The federal judicial hierarchy is primarily composed of three tiers of judges, with the federal trial courts—the U.S. District Courts—occupying the lowest tier. The middle tier is occupied by the U.S. Courts of Appeals,[5] with the U.S. Supreme Court sitting at the apex of the federal judiciary. While the U.S. Supreme Court's geographic jurisdiction covers the entire United States and its territories, the District Courts and Courts of Appeals are organized geographically into districts and circuits.

At the trial court level, there are ninety-four U.S. district courts covering the states, the District of Columbia, and Puerto Rico, with a total of 663 district judgeships.[6] District court boundaries do not cross state lines, and each state has at least one district court, with more populous states having multiple district courts. For example, California, New York, and Texas each have four, while states such as Idaho, Montana, and Nevada each have a single district court. Although every district court has at least two judges, the number of judges serving in each district court also varies, with some district courts having as many as twenty-eight judges.[7] As the major trial courts in the federal system,[8] the U.S. District Courts hear a broad array of civil and criminal cases, with bankruptcy cases handled by special units within each district court.

Appeals from U.S. District Courts are made to the U.S. Courts of Appeals,[9] which are organized into twelve geographic circuits, with a total of 179 judgeships.[10] The U.S. Courts of Appeals also hear appeals from federal administrative agencies, such as the Environmental Protection Agency, the National Labor Relations Board, and the Securities and Exchange Commission. Each circuit consists of an aggregation of district courts and includes district courts from more than one state. The number of states included in a given circuit varies considerably. For example, the Court of Appeals for the Ninth Circuit includes Arizona, Alaska, California, Hawaii, Idaho, Montana, Nevada, Oregon, and Washington, as well as Guam and the Northern Mariana Islands. Twenty-eight judges sit on the Ninth Circuit, with home offices scattered throughout the geographic boundaries of the circuit. Conversely, the Court of Appeals for the First Circuit includes only six judges and three states: Maine, New Hampshire, and Massachusetts, as well as Puerto Rico. The U.S. Courts of Appeals typically decide cases using panels of three judges randomly selected from the total number of judges in the circuit,[11] and appeals from the U.S. Courts of Appeals go directly to the U.S. Supreme Court (see figure 1).

As the major intermediate appellate courts in the federal system, the U.S. Courts of Appeals are enormously important judicial bodies. Unlike the U.S. Supreme Court, which has the discretion to accept or reject appeals through the process of granting or denying the writ of certiorari,[12] the circuit courts have mandatory jurisdiction over most appeals made to them. As a result, judges on the courts of appeals have quite heavy caseloads. For example, in fiscal year 2002, the circuit courts of appeals resolved almost 58,000 appeals, covering most areas of federal law.[13] In contrast, on average, the U.S. Supreme Court has decided fewer than 100 cases with signed opinions per year in the last decade or so.[14] In other

FIGURE 1. Federal judicial system

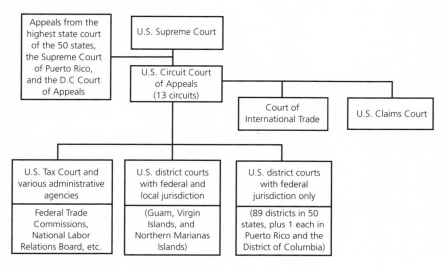

SOURCE: Administrative Office of the United States Courts

words, for every case disposed of by the U.S. Supreme Court, the U.S. Courts of Appeals handle almost 600. Thus, not only are the circuit courts the appellate workhorses of the federal judiciary, but they also serve as the de facto (if not the de jure) court of last resort in the overwhelming majority of appeals.

The fact that the U.S. Courts of Appeals serve in this capacity belies their formally subordinate position in the federal judicial hierarchy. Though the U.S. Supreme Court's declination to review a case appealed to it from the U.S. Courts of Appeals is not the same thing as the Court reviewing and affirming such a case, the lower court ruling remains the final word for litigants in that particular case. More important, until the U.S. Supreme Court explicitly says otherwise, that circuit court ruling remains authoritative precedent for all the federal courts within that circuit's geographic jurisdiction. While there can be and often is substantial agreement across circuits as to appropriate rules of law (Klein 2002), in the absence of action on the part of the U.S. Supreme Court, precedents from one circuit may be persuasive for judges in other circuits but are not binding. Indeed, such a conflict among the circuit courts must be resolved by the Supreme Court to ensure uniformity of national law.

Although the U.S. Supreme Court often captures the public limelight, the U.S. Courts of Appeals arguably constitute *the* appellate tribunal in the federal system. In recognition of both their formal and informal roles, one prominent scholar of the circuit courts has characterized the courts of appeals as "the vital center of the federal judicial system" (Lumbard 1968, 29). These courts are arguably even more important now than when J. Edward Lumbard characterized them as such over twenty years ago. Another influential scholar has argued that, given their varied caseload and the infrequency of Supreme Court review, the courts of appeals constitute "major political institutions that function not only as norm enforcers but also as important creators of public policy" (Songer 1991, 35). In short, the U.S. Courts of Appeals are tremendously significant courts and merit careful study.

Studying these courts is important for another reason beyond their intrinsic significance. Simply put, understanding the U.S. Courts of Appeals can shed light on judicial behavior in other appellate courts. All but eleven states have intermediate appellate courts as part of their judicial systems.[15] And, like the federal circuit courts, many intermediate appellate courts in the states sit to decide cases using panels of judges, creating a similar institutional environment for judges in both systems. Moreover, appellate judges in general—regardless of court system—share many common institutional constraints. In the United States, appellate courts review appeals primarily to identify legal, as opposed to factual, error made in the trial courts. Appellate courts in the United States (and in many other countries) share a norm of deference to the trial courts, especially on matters involving the credibility of witnesses or the sufficiency of the evidence. And most appellate courts throughout the world operate as collegial courts with multijudge panels, thus providing the opportunity for disagreement among the judges. For these reasons, the federal circuit courts provide a useful natural laboratory for the study of appellate court decision making as a generalized phenomenon.

The U.S. Courts of Appeals are also significant public policymakers within the federal governmental system. Public policy has been defined as "the authoritative allocation of values and resources" (Easton 1953, 129). Often scholars and citizens think first of the legislative and executive branches as the primary determiners of public policy, yet clearly the third branch also plays an important role in the allocation of values and resources. Most immediately, the decision a judge renders in any given case allocates resources between the direct parties to that case. Further, whether at the trial or appellate court level, judges allocate values and resources between citizens more broadly either through the enforcement of norms or the development of legal rules that favor one group in society over another

(Mather 1995). Judges also contribute to the determination of societal norms through the interpretation of constitutional and statutory provisions in ways that elevate or shield values such as equality, liberty, and privacy. And while courts may operate in a manner more likely to favor the status quo than to generate social change (Horowitz 1977; Rosenberg 1991), they nevertheless play a central role in determining winners and losers in political, economic, and social interactions. Indeed, some have even argued that courts are the most powerful political force in the nation (Neely 1981; cf. Kozlowski 2003).

Among the most powerful of these courts are the U.S. Courts of Appeals, particularly because (1) they render decisions that serve as precedent in large geographic regions of the United States and its territories, (2) within those regions, they render authoritative interpretations of federal regulatory, statutory, and constitutional law, and (3) those interpretations are authoritative unless and until the Supreme Court intervenes, a relatively rare occurrence. Of course, circuit court judgments must (in theory) be consistent with Supreme Court precedent, but the Court's limited agenda means that the vast majority of circuit court decisions remain unchallenged on appeal.

Several recent cases help illustrate these courts' inherent policymaking power. For example, in 1996, in the case of *Hopwood v. State of Texas,*[16] the Fifth Circuit, with jurisdiction over Texas, Mississippi, and Louisiana, ruled that the University of Texas Law School's admissions program favoring minority applicants through racial preferences violated the Equal Protection Clause of the Fourteenth Amendment. Not only did the *Hopwood* decision generate a powerful ripple throughout institutions of higher education by raising doubts about their admissions programs, but it also had the almost immediate effect of causing a substantial drop in the percentage of minorities enrolled at the University of Texas School of Law. By 1999 the percentage of African Americans in the entering law school class was less than the percentage enrolled in 1950, the year that African Americans were first admitted to the law school (Russell 2000, 507). This circuit court ruling remained in place for seven years, until the Supreme Court decided *Grutter v. Bollinger*[17] in 2003 and superseded the *Hopwood* holding with its own analysis of affirmative action. For a seven-year period, therefore, the circuit court ruling influenced the educational prospects of thousands of African American applicants in at least three populous states.

In addition to *Hopwood,* consider the case of *Flynt v. Rumsfeld,* decided by the D.C. Circuit in 2004.[18] In *Flynt,* magazine publisher Larry Flynt sued the secretary of defense, challenging a Defense Department directive controlling media access to troops in combat operations in Afghanistan. Flynt claimed that the Defense Department's limitations on magazine reporters' access to troops engaged in special operations violated his First Amendment rights. Although the D.C. Circuit held that Flynt had standing to challenge the directive, it further concluded that no First Amendment right existed for the media to be "embedded" with combat troops. Rather, it found that the Defense Department's directive was a reasonable "time, place, and manner" restriction on such access and did not represent an unconstitutional infringement on First Amendment rights. Clearly, the D.C. Circuit's decision in this case has significant policy implications for media coverage of wartime operations by the U.S. military.

Dissensus, Consensus, and Judicial Policymaking

As the preceding discussions illustrate, the U.S. Courts of Appeals play an important policymaking role. More important for this book, they also suggest that judges must decide politically sensitive questions that implicate fundamental values such as liberty or equality. Resolving such issues—even in the judicial forum—often requires judges to look for guidance beyond legal texts to their own policy preferences. We began this chapter with a story about Juan Ramirez-Lopez and the power of dissent. In that case, Judge Kozinski's dissent found no explicit legal or factual error in the district court's judgment. Instead, Kozinski relied on broader principles of justice (spiced with a little sarcasm) to persuade the government to release Mr. Ramirez-Lopez. The political nature of judicial decision making is manifest, in part, because it causes judges to rely on their personal sense of justice when deciding some appeals. The empirical dynamics of judicial decision making also reveal that judges do far more than simply mechanically apply law to resolve disputes. In particular, dissensus among judges, whether among members of an appellate panel or between judges at different levels in a judicial hierarchy, often reflects conflict over the values inherent in different policy alternatives and indicates that judges are not always "bound" by existing precedent or other legal rules in determining case outcomes (see Songer 1986). In this regard, dissensus constitutes an important indicator of the political nature of judicial decision making.

It is no surprise, then, that most political scientists interested in the policymaking dynamics on the bench have focused their attention on nonunanimous opinions, especially when constructing models of judicial voting behavior. According to one prominent scholar of the federal appeals courts, such nonunanimous opinions reflect "choice situations sufficient to alter the outcomes, while other cases do not" (Goldman 1969, 217; see also Atkins and Green, 1976). In the context of state supreme courts, Melinda Gann Hall and Paul Brace have similarly noted that "[t]he willingness of judges to express disagreement openly with their court majorities presents a striking challenge to the notion that legal doctrines adequately explain the judicial vote and also provides important opportunities to assess the motivations and influences underlying judicial choice" (1999, 286).

These existing studies generally evaluate dissensus between individual judges on appellate panels in the form of dissenting and concurring opinions. As noted previously, we refer to this as horizontal dissensus, because it concerns disagreement among judges within the same hierarchical level in the judiciary. Conversely, vertical dissensus occurs when judges at different levels of the judicial system disagree with one other. The most obvious manifestation of this form of dissensus involves reversals of a lower court. In this book, we evaluate both manifestations of dissensus on the U.S. Courts of Appeals in recognition of their importance in terms of the processing of cases, judicial outcomes, and the development of the law.

In addition to viewing vertical and horizontal dissensus as separate elements, it is also important to reflect on the relationship between intercourt and intracourt dissensus. Reversal may spark conflict on the appellate panel itself by generating a dissent there—what Burton Atkins calls "the contagion of conflict" (1990, 96). Reversal may also produce "more subtle forms of conflict," including concurring votes or opinions (Atkins 1990, 77). In our own research, we have found that when the appellate panel reverses the trial court, a dissent or concurrence is more likely (Hettinger, Lindquist, and Martinek 2003c). In the three circuits he studied, Howard (1981) similarly found a relationship between reversal and dissent, with an approximately seven-percentage point difference in the rate of dissent in affirming and reversing cases. Atkins (1990) reports the same relationship. Thus, vertical and horizontal dissensus are not independent phenomena, but rather reflect a broader dynamic of disagreement within panels and between tiers of the judicial hierarchy. We seek to evaluate the connection between vertical and horizontal dissensus in the chapters that follow.

Horizontal Dissensus

We begin our investigation by seeking to identify the determinants of horizontal dissensus as reflected by judicial voting behavior on three-judge circuit court panels.[19] Decision making on rotating circuit court panels composed of three judges is governed by majority rule, and thus one judge may dissent from the two-judge majority. Whether or not there is a dissenting opinion, there may also be a concurring opinion. Hence, a single case may result in three written opinions: a majority opinion, a concurring opinion, and a dissenting opinion.[20]

An appellate judge may express disagreement with the majority's resolution of a case in several ways. First, she may file an opinion expressing her dissent from the majority's conclusion in whole or in part. Occasionally, a judge may dissent without opinion, but this occurs only rarely.[21] Judges can dissent for any number of reasons, including (1) when the dissenter believes the majority has made a serious mistake on a significant legal issue that is likely to recur; (2) when the dissenter believes the majority has made an erroneous factual assessment; or (3) when the dissenter feels that the controlling legal rule or precedent is unjust (Coffin 1994, 227–28).[22] In addition, a judge may choose to concur rather than dissent. Although a concurrence is not as clear a signal of disagreement with the majority as a dissent, it does reflect at least some level of dissatisfaction with the majority's resolution of the case. While a concurring judge agrees with the ultimate outcome endorsed by the majority (i.e., a decision for or against the appellant), such a judge may nevertheless concur for a variety of reasons. She may wish to register her preference for a different legal theory or grounds to support the result. Alternatively, she may wish to identify limitations in the majority's opinion. Or, she may see a concurrence as an opportunity to attempt to expand the majority's reasoning on a particular point (Coffin 1994, 228).

The expression of dissent (or the rendering of a concurrence) can provide judges with the satisfaction derived from directly expressing their preferences. As Justice Antonin Scalia has noted,

> To be able to write an opinion solely for oneself, without the need to accommodate, to any degree whatever, the more-or-less differing views of one's colleagues; to address precisely the points of law that one considers important and *no others;* to express precisely the degree of quibble, or foreboding, or disbelief, or indication that one believes the majority's disposition should engender—that is indeed an unparalleled pleasure (1994, 42, emphasis in original).

Dissents may also preserve individual judges' independence, as it allows them to express their disagreement through a legitimate channel. Justice Scalia also argues that "a signed majority opinion, opposed by one or more signed dissents, makes it clear that these decisions are the product of independent and thoughtful minds" (Scalia 1994, 35). Dissent can serve a palliative function as well, because it may reduce judges' "cognitive dissonance" and frustration (Peterson 1981, 428 and 431).

Dissents provide institutional benefits, too. A dissent "safeguards the integrity of the judicial decision-making process by keeping the majority accountable for the rationale and consequences of its decision" (Brennan 1986, 430). Indeed, Justice William Brennan defended dissents, because they create an adversarial crucible from which the most solidly forged rule of law is most likely to emerge. Further, dissents may foreshadow trends or developments in the law, as did Justice John Marshall Harlan's dissent in *Plessy v. Ferguson.* Harlan's dissent admonished, "Our Constitution is color-blind, and neither knows nor tolerates classes among citizens,"[23] thereby foreshadowing the Court's later rulings in race discrimination. Such dissents play an important role in doctrinal evolution. And in the rare instance, a dissent may also persuade the parties to reach a just settlement. The case described at the beginning of this chapter, *United States v. Ramirez-Lopez,* provides an example of such an effective dissent (see Fisher 2003).

However, judges who choose to dissent or concur have their critics. Dissensus obviously undermines consensual decision-making processes, and consensual decision making on appellate courts serves critical institutional interests. For example, unanimity among judges may promote institutional legitimacy and effective implementation of individual decisions by providing a unified voice behind judicial policies. Judge Learned Hand, a distinguished jurist who served on the Court of Appeals for the Second Circuit, suggested that a dissent "cancels the impact of monolithic solidarity on which the authority of a bench of judges so largely depends" (Hand 1958, 72). In other words, "[t]he avoidance of overt dissension may be imperative to mobilize political and public support behind new or controversial court policy and ultimately to obtain compliance" (Goldman and Lamb 1986, 1). Consensual decision making helps promote the perception that the law is *not* political in nature—and thus subject to the influence of individual judges—but rather is uniformly and impartially applied. Such a perception may aid in enhancing compliance with court decisions. The public's acceptance of the rule of law, therefore, hinges to some degree on citizens' belief that the law is not shaped by judges' personal predilections; judicial consensus is more likely to enhance that perception.

Second, consensual decision making promotes the efficient adminis-

tration of justice, because conflict among judges interferes with the or-
derly disposition of a court's caseload. Dissenting opinions usually mean
more work for the judges on the panel, not only for the dissenter herself,
who must expend a scarce resource (time) to craft the separate opinion,
but also for those in the majority who may feel the need to counter the
dissenter's arguments (Flanders 1999, 402). Separate opinions—or their
absence—affect efficiency in yet another way. When judges march in
lockstep, citizens and their lawyers are better able to predict the outcome
of legal disputes that may reach the courts and thus are more likely to
settle their disputes without recourse to litigation. Dissents make the law
less certain, and frequent dissents are likely to increase a court's caseload
because lawyers are sensitive to uncertainty on the court (manifested in
dissents or concurrences) and thus may press litigation in those areas of
uncertainty (Peterson 1981, 425).

The preceding discussion focuses on the *impact* or *consequences* of
horizontal dissensus, both individually and institutionally. These considerations largely rest on normative considerations, though clearly some of
the dimensions discussed above may be assessed empirically. Concern
over the detrimental consequences of dissensus became most pronounced, however, in the second half of the twentieth century, when separate opinion writing became commonplace rather than rare (Kadzielski
and Kunda 1983; Haynie 1992). At the U.S. Supreme Court, as well as in
state and lower federal appellate courts, the 1930s and 1940s marked the
emergence of a new pattern of dissensus on these courts (Songer, Sheehan, and Haire 2000, 106–7). Although it is unclear why these patterns
changed over time, in the modern era, the filing of separate opinions has
become far more acceptable on appellate courts. In this book, we do not
analyze the impact of dissents or concurrences or their normative justifications; rather, we analyze what causes judges to dissent or concur. Why
would an individual judge risk judicial collegiality and consensus to express disagreement with the majority opinion, even in light of the positive
normative benefits some commentators have associated with dissents?

Vertical Dissensus

In 1967 Richard Richardson and Kenneth Vines cautioned against
viewing elements of the judicial hierarchy in isolation. Without evaluating the judicial decision-making process in interactional terms, they
wrote, we can learn little about "power relationships within and between
courts" (598). "The federal judicial system . . . articulates as a system"

(Frankfurter and Landis 1927, 3). Hence, important disagreement among judges is not limited to appellate judges serving on the same reviewing panel. The U.S. Courts of Appeals sit as the central tier of the federal judicial hierarchy and bear responsibility for reviewing and monitoring the decisions of the federal district courts. In doing so, circuit judges correct legal or technical errors made in the lower courts by reversing the lower court judgment. They also confirm the proper interpretation and application of the law when they affirm the judgment below. Since appellate review in the U.S. Courts of Appeals is not discretionary, error correction constitutes an important function of appellate panels.[24]

But error correction in the sense of correcting technical errors on the part of lower court judges is not the only form of error correction in which courts of appeals jurists engage. Appellate judges also correct error in the sense of ensuring that the decisions of lower courts comport with the policies articulated in appellate court precedent. Some scholars have suggested that the primary function of the appellate process is to formulate policy (cf. Landes and Posner 1979). Policymaking is inevitable in the appellate review process, because the disposition of any given case reflects the applicable legal rules for the resolution of future disputes (Haire, Lindquist, and Songer 2003; Richardson and Vines 1967).

Disagreement between the two lower tiers of the federal judicial system is most clearly manifested when the appellate court reverses the judgment of the lower court. As Richardson and Vines have observed:

> [A]mong the many opportunities available in the judicial system for the potential eruption of conflict, that of reversing a decision by one judge over another is especially dramatic. It calls for a much more deliberate act on the part of the individual judge than would be the case when simply affirming the action of a colleague. It necessitates rationalizing of conflict in proper terms, discounting the arguments honored in the lower court and posing alternative values. . . . Reversal is therefore not just a disagreement; it is an exceptional assertive expression of lack of confidence in the lower court judge (1967, 604).

Other observers, including federal judges themselves, have acknowledged the interpersonal tensions that can arise between appellate and trial court judges "borne of the structural relationship in which they both function" (Newman 1992, 629; see also Coffin 1994). Burton Atkins has referred to appellate court disruption of lower court judgments as an "intervention," whereby the appellate court "alters, reshapes or entirely reverses the decision made by a lower forum" (1990, 72–73). In particular, the appellate court may reverse the lower court judgment in whole or in part, vacate the decision below, and/or remand for additional proceedings in light of the appellate court's mandate. Such interventions inject "overt, visible conflict into the judicial hierarchy," but they also have more far-reaching effects, including enhancing the likelihood of upper court review (Caldeira, Wright, and Zorn 1999), increasing workload burdens, and creating the perception of instability in the law (Songer, Sheehan, and Haire 2000, 53).[25]

REVERSAL AND THE DISTRICT COURT JUDGE. From the perspective of a district court judge, reversal is likely to be something she wishes to avoid for several reasons. First, judges are human beings and, as such, generally prefer to encounter approval rather than disapproval, all things being equal. Reversal of a district court judge by a panel of circuit court judges does not always signify overt disapproval of the former by the latter. Indeed, there are any number of instances in which courts of appeals judges have gone out of their way to make clear that a reversal should not be construed as admonishing the district court judge in any sense. For example, in reversing Judge Gene Carter in *U.S. v. Griffin,* the First Circuit opinion included the following footnote: "It should not be implied that we have any fault to find with the trial judge's resolution of the problem."[26] And even though the three-judge panel reviewing Judge Michael Mukasey's decision denying a defendant's claims that the jury selection process was discriminatory unanimously disagreed with his decision, in his majority opinion Circuit Judge Richard Cardamone referred to Judge Mukasey as a "respected district court judge."[27] Nonetheless, no matter what reason is given for the reversal and no matter how congenial the language used, a reversal is still not the same thing as an affirmance.

Further, having one's decisions reversed with any degree of regularity has the potential for impact well beyond any case immediately at hand. Evan Caminker suggests that judges will see a pattern of reversal as compromising their professional opportunities in two ways. First, judges "fear that their professional audience, including colleagues, practitioners, and scholars, will disrespect their legal judgments or abilities" (1994, 77). Though judges' concern for their reputations typically receives cursory attention by scholars, it is not a trivial matter for judges. This is not to say that there has been no scholarly attention to issues of judicial reputation. Rather, the difficulty in developing an operational definition of judicial reputation that is both valid and amenable to empirical measurement has led many scholars to acknowledge its potential importance but then go on to omit it from any systematic study. One notable exception is recent work by David Klein and Darby Morrisroe (1999), in which the authors develop a measure of prestige based on counts of references to judges' names by other judges and then use this measure to investigate the influence of prestige on the adoption of novel legal rules.[28]

What this research suggests is that, even if a judge had no intrinsic interest in developing a reputation for being a good judge for its own sake, a judge wishing to influence the decision making of other judges— whether to induce other judges to behave in ways that comport with the judge's policy preferences or to encourage other judges to behave in ways that reflect good legal policy as that judge sees it—will be concerned for his reputation. And, hence, he will remain cognizant of the potential for reversals to damage that reputation.

Caminker (1994) further suggests that judges will be concerned with reversals because they impinge on reputational issues for another reason: a desire for advancement. Scholars studying the Supreme Court pay virtually no attention to issues of progressive ambition on the part of Supreme Court justices, other than to mention that justices are unlikely to harbor the desire for some other position (Rohde and Spaeth 1976; Segal and Spaeth 1993, 2002).[29] Given the location of the Supreme Court at the apex of the federal judiciary and the esteem in which the institution is held, this is entirely appropriate. With regard to courts of appeals judges, the desire for elevation to the Supreme Court may be there, but the chances for such advancement are slim to none. Given that there are 179 authorized courts of appeals judgeships and nine members of the Supreme Court, there are almost twenty circuit court judges for every seat on the Supreme Court. Of course, that is not to say that a circuit court judge cannot dream! But the consequences of reversal for the chances of promotion (via the impact on judicial reputation) are likely to matter more for district court judges, who have a much more reasonable chance of elevation to the U.S. Courts of Appeals. There are 663 authorized district court judgeships, which means that there are fewer than four district court judges for every seat on the courts of appeals.

Certainly, members of the courts of appeals are not the only pool of potential candidates for the Supreme Court and district court judges are not the only viable candidates for the courts of appeals. But these numbers make clear that district court judges are likely to be much more sanguine about their prospects for elevation to the circuit bench than courts of appeals judges about their prospects for elevation to the Supreme Court bench. To borrow a framework developed by Lawrence Baum, both circuit and district court judges are likely to have the inherent goal of elevation to a higher bench. But not all inherent goals become operative goals. "Of the various inherent goals that individual judges hold, some may be irrelevant to their work as judges" (Baum 1997, 14). Hence, while both circuit and district court judges might have the desire for elevation, the opportunity for elevation is practically nonexistent for the former, so the inherent goal of elevation is not readily translated into an operative goal. This means that, while neither circuit court nor district court judges are likely to be fond of being reversed, the latter are more likely to care about reversal because of its potential effect on achieving the goal of elevation.

District court judges are unlikely to welcome reversal for reasons beyond reputational costs of the kind discussed above. For example, a more mundane reason district court judges may see reversal as less than desirable has to do with their workloads. Reversals entail more work. Granted, some reversals, such as those that reverse and remand, create more work than others. Nevertheless, most impose at least some demands on already-busy judges. Further, reversal is likely to be distasteful to district court judges because they are legal actors who have arguably undergone a socialization process that encourages them to value arriving at the legally sound decision. "Many judges want to 'get it right' simply because they have internalized norms of stare decisis through their professional training and because judicial decisions must be rationalized on the basis of precedent" (Haire, Lindquist, and Songer 2003, 147).

District court judges might also want to "get it right" for yet another reason. If district court judges care about policy, as the extant evidence suggests that they do (e.g., Carp and Rowland 1983; Richardson and Vines 1970; Rowland and Carp 1996), then presumably they would prefer not to be reversed by their respective court of appeals to avoid having the policy embedded in the lower court ruling "undone." "Given their position at the bottom of the federal judicial hierarchy, one might argue that . . . the policy-making *powers* of federal trial courts are constrained by the power of appellate courts to reverse their judgments. [And] [t]o some degree this is true" (Rowland 1991, 65). But that does not mean that district court judges are entirely shut out of the policymaking that inheres in judging. Although a district court decision in a given case constitutes an authoritative resolution only for the litigants in that particular case, it nonetheless is an authoritative resolution that, as part of a pattern of such resolutions, creates policy. Reversals, then, threaten to modify or invalidate that policy.

Despite the fact that reversals may only rarely be accompanied by opinions publicly dressing down erroneous lower court judges—and, indeed, are not infrequently accompanied by opinions that are quite careful not to criticize the lower court judge—there are any number of reasons that district court judges are likely to look askance at reversals by the courts of appeals. Whether because of reputational, workload, or policy reasons, reversal is unlikely to be welcomed by a district court judge and, hence, has the very real potential to fray collegial relations with circuit court judges.

REVERSAL AND THE CIRCUIT COURT. As the individuals with the authority to review and possibly reverse district court rulings, circuit court judges are apt to see reversals differently. Reversal is really the only tool at the disposal of the circuit to correct errant lower court rulings. At root, the decision by an appeals court panel whether or not to reverse the decision of a district court judge uncovers a tension between two (potentially) competing goals: correcting error and assuring collegiality. With regard to error correction, the "error" may be legal error or policy error, as noted earlier. The former involves identifying and correctly applying the relevant legal principles. The latter involves compliance with the policy preferences of superior judges in the judicial system.

Error correction in the sense of ensuring the correct application of legal principles is inherent in the hierarchical nature of the judiciary. In other words, the very design of the federal judicial system is predicated on the notion that higher courts will review lower courts as a mechanism for assuring fairness (at least procedural fairness) in the legal system. "[T]rial courts make mistakes, and appellate courts, because of their greater expertise, lesser time pressures, collegial decision making, or some other reason, correct those mistakes" (Drahozal 1998, 469). This does not mean that the U.S. Courts of Appeals can—or even should—correct every lower court error. A fundamental appellate principle is the distinction between harmless and reversible error. Harmless error is legal error that makes no difference as to the outcome in a case, that is, error that does not compromise the rights of a litigant (American Bar Association 1994). Harmless error does not require reversal. Reversible error, however, is error that demands correction by a reviewing court because it somehow infringes on litigant rights.[30]

Error correction in the sense of ensuring deference to the policy prescriptions embedded in the decisions of the circuit has received considerable attention in the scholarly literature on judicial impact and compliance. Generally, researchers have found that the rulings of inferior courts follow those of their superiors—that is, the ideological trends in higher courts appear to influence the ideological trends of lower courts (Songer, Segal, and Cameron 1994; Benesh 2002) and higher court precedents influence the decisions of lower courts (Songer and Sheehan 1990; Songer and Haire 1992). More recent work focusing directly on the congruence between district court and circuit court preferences found that the greater the congruence in ideological preferences between the two, the less likely is reversal (Haire, Lindquist, and Songer 2003). Given that the available evidence indicates that courts of appeals judges are policy-oriented actors (e.g., Goldman 1975; Howard 1981; Songer and Haire 1992),[31] this is hardly surprising.

Whether circuit judges are concerned with error correction in the legal or policy sense, reversal is the only meaningful recourse a circuit panel has to "correct" the lower court: circuit court judges learn "from long and frustrating experience that one reversal is worth a hundred lectures" (Coffin 1994, 163). While it is true that district courts formally occupy a position inferior to the courts of appeals in the federal judicial hierarchy, district court judges are not beholden to circuit court judges either for securing their positions originally or retaining them subsequently. Neither their working conditions nor their remuneration depend on their circuit court superiors. That leaves reversal (or the threat thereof). David Klein and Robert Hume (2003) recently demonstrated the tenuousness of claims regarding the fear of reversal as a tool for the U.S. Supreme Court to induce compliance on the part of the U.S. Courts of Appeals. But, as discussed above, there is good reason to suspect that reversal is much more of a meaningful sanction for district courts than for courts of appeals. Further, Susan Haire, Stefanie Lindquist, and Donald Songer (2003) provide empirical evidence to buttress the claim that reversal matters for district court judges. Whether reversal is used as a tool to assure "correct" legal decision making or ideological obedience, its exercise is unlikely to be taken lightly and has the potential, whether that potential is realized or not, to generate a rift in collegial relations between these two important levels of the federal judiciary.

Like horizontal dissensus, then, vertical dissensus has important implications for the efficacy of a court system and for the stability and predictability of the law. The normative implications are clear, as are the implications of reversal for relations between the trial and appeals courts. In light of these adverse consequences, under what conditions will appeals courts be most likely to reverse? One might assume, for example, that appellate judges will reverse only reluctantly to avoid injustice or correct clear error. In this book, we seek to assess the determinants of this critical function of the appellate courts in the federal judicial hierarchy.

Conclusion

Dissensus both among judges serving on a three-judge panel at the U.S. Courts of Appeals and between the U.S. District Courts and the U.S. Courts of Appeals have consequences both for immediate litigants and for shaping the legal landscape. Their importance in these regards demands close investigation to identify the determinants of disagreements within circuits. In the next chapter, we examine theoretical perspectives on decision making in appellate courts, paying special attention to attitudinal and institutional theories of how judges make decisions. Our ultimate purpose there is to develop a realistic account of the factors that are likely to prompt the expression of horizontal and vertical dissensus. In chapter 3, we conduct an empirical investigation of the decision to file a separate opinion on the U.S. Courts of Appeals, focusing on how various characteristics of judges, cases, and circuits structure the decisions that are made. We consider strategic considerations in the choice to dissent in chapter 4. In particular, we explore whether U.S. Courts of Appeals judges use dissenting opinions as mechanisms for inviting *en banc* proceedings and/or Supreme Court review. Chapter 5 focuses on the dynamics underlying the decision to overturn a district court decision. In the concluding chapter, we consider the implications of our empirical findings.

TWO

Theoretical Perspectives on Decision Making in Appellate Courts

An enormous amount of scholarly time and energy has been devoted to unraveling the puzzle of judicial behavior. Given the important role judges play both in the resolution of particular disputes and in the development of public policy, scholarly fascination with judicial decision making comes as no surprise. The controversial and political nature of U.S. Supreme Court decision making is certainly not something that is newly apparent. For example, the laissez-faire philosophy of the Supreme Court during the Great Depression put it squarely at odds with President Franklin Delano Roosevelt's New Deal, nearly resulting in a constitutional crisis when the president sought to increase the size of the Court to enable him to appoint justices sympathetic to his legislative agenda (Garbus 2003). Further, the Supreme Court's controversial rulings with regard to the rights of the criminally accused during the heyday of the Warren Court brought down a rain of criticisms from numerous quarters (Powe 2001). More recently, the Court's ruling in *Bush v. Gore* emphasized the political dimension of judging by demonstrating that even the outcome of a presidential election may hinge on a ruling by that court.[1]

As pointed out in the previous chapter, the political nature of adjudication is also evident in the decision making of lower courts. A good example is the Ninth Circuit decision in *Newdow v. U.S. Congress,* in which the appellate panel agreed that the Elk Grove Unified School District's policy requiring teacher-led recitation of the Pledge of Allegiance violated the Establishment Clause of the First Amendment.[2] Though the original version of the pledge did not contain religious references, the version codified by Congress in 1954 includes the phrase: "one nation under God."[3] Michael Newdow, an avowed atheist, whose daughter attended elementary school in the Elk Grove Unified School District, argued that the recitation of the pledge every day by his daughter's teacher and classmates represented a violation of the First Amendment, even though his daughter was not compelled to participate in reciting the pledge. The original three-judge panel hearing the appeal agreed. When a majority of the entire membership of the circuit chose not to rehear the case, Ninth Circuit judges on both sides of the debate issued separate opinions. Expressions of public outrage followed both the original decision and the circuit decision not to rehear the case, including statements by President George W. Bush (Foskett 2002) and Supreme Court justice Antonin Scalia (Salmon 2003) as well as unanimous condemnation by the U.S. Senate (Firestone 2003). Subsequently, the original panel stayed enforcement of its own ruling, and the Supreme Court granted certiorari in 2003.[4]

In another illustrative case, this time from the federal trial court level, Judge Harold Baer Jr. of the U.S. District Court for the Southern District of New York, suppressed evidence—including thirty-four kilograms of cocaine and two kilograms of heroin—in Carol Bayless's 1996 criminal trial for conspiracy to distribute drugs. Bayless had been arrested in New York City during the early morning hours one day in April of 1995 while either the driver of (according to police officers) or a passenger in (according to Bayless) an out-of-state rental car. After weighing the testimony of the arresting officer and Ms. Bayless's videotaped statement made to police after her arrest, Judge Baer concluded that the police lacked "reasonable suspicion the defendant was engaged in criminal activity" when they searched the car.[5] The subsequent political outcry was both swift and strident. President Bill Clinton expressed regret at appointing Baer (Van Natta 1996) and Senate Majority Leader (and then Republican presidential candidate) Bob Dole argued for Baer's impeachment (Groner 1996). The criticism of Baer's ruling was so intense that four circuit judges from the Second Circuit, including the current and three former chief judges of the circuit, issued a public statement characterizing the criticisms as having gone too far ("Judges: Attacks on Baer Go Too Far" 1996). Ultimately, Judge Baer reversed his own decision a scant three months later.[6]

The cases of Michael Newdow and Carol Bayless illustrate that adjudication in the U.S. Courts of Appeals and the U.S. District Courts is clearly political in nature. Policymaking is inherent in the process of judging: "Everyone professionally involved with law knows that . . . judges . . . make law, only more cautiously, more slowly, and in a more principled, less partisan, fashion than legislators" (Posner 1995, 235). Because of the important policy consequences of judicial decisions, whether at the trial or appellate level, scholars have attempted to develop theories or models of judicial decision making in an effort to explain and predict why judges do what they do. Models of judicial decision making are simplified depictions of reality that allow observers to make broad generalizations about the key determinants of such behavior for most judges, without getting bogged down in the idiosyncratic characteristics or actions of individual judges. In other words, a theory of judicial behavior—like any theory—is intended to account for the general patterns we can discern in that behavior. We begin our discussion with the very prominent attitudinal model of judicial behavior, which has been quite useful in explaining general patterns in appellate judges' decisions. As explained below, the attitudinal model, which focuses on the politicized nature of judicial decision making, differs substantially from a vision of judges as neutral adjudicators who rely solely on the written law to determine case outcomes. Once we have the attitudinal model firmly in hand, we can elaborate on it to account for nonattitudinal factors that are likely to shape judicial behavior, such as the choice of a circuit judge to author a separate opinion or the decision of a reviewing appellate panel to reverse a district court ruling.

THE ATTITUDINAL MODEL. Until the twentieth century, most lawyers and scholars believed that judging was a mechanistic enterprise in which judges applied the law and rendered decisions without recourse to their own ideological or policy preferences. This formalistic conception of law, perhaps most closely associated with Christopher Columbus Langdell at Harvard, held that law constituted a set of objective norms that, if analyzed using proper methods, would allow judges to reach "objective, determinate [and] impersonal" decisions (Posner 1990, 7; see also Duxbury 1995, chapter 1). In the 1920s, however, a group of jurists and legal philosophers, known collectively as "legal realists," recognized that judicial discretion was quite broad and that often the law did not mandate a particular result. Legal realism, of which Justice Oliver Wendell Holmes Jr. was arguably the earliest proponent, took root at the Columbia and University of Chicago Law Schools.[7] Among the most prominent of the legal realists were Karl Llewellyn and Jerome Frank. Llewellyn was a Yale-trained lawyer and legal scholar who enjoyed a prestigious corporate law career before joining the faculty of, successively, the Yale, Columbia, and University of Chicago Law Schools. Frank, a distinguished jurist who served almost sixteen years on the U.S. Court of Appeals for the Second

Circuit, received his legal training from the University of Chicago Law School.

There were really two distinct schools of thought within the legal realism movement, one that emphasized social forces and another that focused on individual judge characteristics. Both saw the law as indeterminate, since often there is more than one legitimate legal basis for arriving at a decision and thus no necessarily unique outcome dictated by the "law." The sociological variant of legal realism, of which Llewellyn was an advocate, focused on social forces (like professional socialization) as determinants of judicial decisions. The second variant, and the one for which Frank was better known, saw the characteristics of individual judges as most important. In its most extreme formulation, the realist perspective suggests that the law is simply what judges decide when settling disputes.[8] According to the legal realists, focusing on this "law in action" was far more useful for understanding law and its implementation than focusing exclusively on the "law on the books" (Duxbury 1995, 67–68). Most fundamentally, the legal realists drew our attention to the fact that lawmaking is inherent in judging (Segal and Spaeth 2002, 87–88).

The attitudinal model of judicial decision making traces its roots to legal realism. Drawing on the intellectual foundation laid by the legal realists, later scholars (Pritchett 1948, 1954; Schubert 1965; Rohde and Spaeth 1976) developed theories of judicial behavior that explicitly acknowledged the political nature of judging and accounted for the influence of judges' values on their actions. The attitudinal model's two most well-known contemporary advocates, Jeffrey A. Segal and Harold J. Spaeth, describe the model as follows: "This model holds that the Supreme Court decides disputes in light of the facts of the case vis-à-vis the ideological attitudes and values of the justices. Simply put, Rehnquist votes the way he does because he is extremely conservative; Marshall voted the way he did because he was extremely liberal" (2002, 86).

The attitudinal model's utility for understanding the decisions of U.S. Supreme Court justices is by now firmly established (e.g., Pritchett 1941; Schubert 1962, 1965; Segal and Spaeth 1993, 2002). However, as Segal and Spaeth have made clear, the key to understanding the attitudinal model's applicability to the Supreme Court is recognizing that the Court's rather unique institutional features impose few constraints on the translation of policy preferences into justices' votes (2002, 92–96).

First, the Supreme Court has virtually autonomous control over its docket. The few exceptions include a limited number of cases arising under the Court's original jurisdiction[9] and appeals from three-judge district courts.[10] Hence, the kinds of cases the Court does hear are those that raise important policy questions, the very kind of cases in which preferences are likely to matter most. Members of the Supreme Court also enjoy lifetime tenure, obviating any concerns about remaining in office.[11] Further, given the prestige and importance of the U.S. Supreme Court, justices generally lack ambition for higher office.[12] Finally, the Supreme Court is *the* court of last resort, meaning its decisions are not subject to review by a higher court. Of course, in matters of statutory interpretation, Congress may reverse what it views to be an erroneous construction on the part of the Court. Evidence that the U.S. Supreme Court is sensitive to such concerns is limited and mixed, however.[13]

The distinctive institutional features of the Supreme Court have led many scholars to question the applicability of the attitudinal model to other courts. At the U.S. Courts of Appeals—unlike at the Supreme Court—circuit court judges are faced with mandatory dockets, and their decisions are subject to review by a higher court, although circuit judges do enjoy life tenure and protection from diminution in their salaries like their brethren on the Supreme Court. Even so, systematic evidence demonstrates that the ideological or policy preferences of judges influence behavior on the U.S. Courts of Appeals as well. In early studies relying on partisan identification as a surrogate measure of circuit judges' policy preferences, researchers consistently found outcomes in the courts of appeals to be determined, at least in significant part, by judges' preferences (Goldman 1966, 1975; Songer 1982). For example, in their longitudinal examination of courts of appeals decision making in several areas of law (labor relations, criminal appeals, First Amendment issues, civil rights), Donald Songer and Sue Davis (1990) found Democratic judges more likely to render liberal decisions than their Republican counterparts.

Further, in examining decision making on the U.S. Courts of Appeals in obscenity cases, Songer and Susan Haire (1992) found partisanship—especially in conjunction with region, another characteristic of judges associated with ideological preferences[14]—influential in judicial choice, despite controlling for the characteristics of litigants and case facts. Even when the influence of Supreme Court precedent is taken into account, existing studies continue to find that decision making on the U.S. Courts of Appeals is shaped by the policy preferences of circuit judges (e.g., Songer, Segal, and Cameron 1994; Reddick 1997; Benesh 2002).

FACTORS BEYOND JUDICIAL ATTITUDES. To say that judges' policy preferences matter in the disposition of cases is not, of course, tantamount to saying that they are the *only* influence that matters. By its very nature as a simplified version of reality, the attitudinal model presents a narrow portrait of judges' behavior. Nevertheless, the attitudinal model constitutes a useful starting point for understanding judicial behavior in the U.S. Courts of Appeals. In this book, therefore, we begin with the assumption that judges are motivated to embody their policy preferences in the law, if possible, an assumption that is amply supported by existing research (e.g., Songer 1991; Songer and Haire 1992). We also recognize, however, that judging is not determined by attitudinal preferences alone. Starting with the attitudinal model as the baseline, we can introduce additional complexity to the model by recognizing the existence of other factors that can influence judicial behavior, such as separate opinion authorship and lower court reversal. We can roughly group these factors into three broad categories: characteristics of judges, characteristics of cases, and characteristics of circuits.

CHARACTERISTICS OF JUDGES. Obviously, the attitudinal preferences of judges are characteristics of judges. But there are other, nonattitudinal characteristics that can lay claim to influencing judicial behavior. One such characteristic is the judge's institutional role or position on the court, which may affect judges' reactions to situations and circumstances arising on the bench. For example, chief judges assume unique administrative responsibilities within their respective circuits and within the federal judicial hierarchy well beyond that of the other circuit judges. There is no official institutional reflection of a chief judge's position with regard to decision making or behavior. In other words, chief judges have few, if any, tools at their disposal to bend their fellow appeals court judges to their will. Yet qualitative and quantitative evidence demonstrates that chief judges engage in behaviors that are different from their nonchief peers and that reflect concern for the institutional functioning of the circuit (Howard 1981; Feinberg 1984; Hettinger, Lindquist, and Martinek 2003b).

Another example of the potential effect of institutional role is the recently appointed judge. Whether it is because these freshman judges feel compelled to defer to other judges on matters before the panel, lack ideological certainty, or struggle with the enormity of their workloads, newer judges manifest behavioral differences. Freshman judges demonstrate less predictability in terms of ideological outcomes (Snyder 1958; but see Heck and Hall 1981) and exhibit lower opinion production (Wood, Keith, Lanier, and Ogundele 1998). Further evidence suggests that freshman judges at the courts of appeals are less likely to dissent from majority opinions (Hettinger, Lindquist, and Martinek 2003a). In addition, other judges sitting on appellate panels on a temporary basis may be less inclined to dissent. Frequently, chief judges appoint district court judges to appellate panels to provide those judges with appellate experience and to reduce workload pressures at the appeals court level.[15] Such temporary appointments can create role conflict for these judges, which may influence their choice to dissent or to reverse the lower court judge.

While judges occupy different formally and informally defined roles at the U.S. Courts of Appeals, it is also true that judges ascend to the circuit court bench with different background experiences and qualifications. In some regards those appointed to the U.S. Courts of Appeals are quite similar. For instance, by custom and tradition, contemporary appointees all have had the benefit of formal legal training. But in other important ways, circuit judges arrive at the bench with unique experiences that have the potential to shape their approach to their work. For example, some become courts of appeals judges with the benefit of previous federal court experience. Some become courts of appeals judges after having served on other, usually state, appellate courts. Previous experience of this type is likely to be consequential for the behavior of judges on the bench. With respect to dissensus, for example, one might expect that judges with prior appellate court experience may be more comfortable with expressing dissent or reversing the lower court judge.

CHARACTERISTICS OF CASES. Judges vary but so, too, do cases. Each case presents a unique set of facts and circumstances. Moreover, the nature of the U.S. Courts of Appeals' mandatory docket means that a significant proportion of the cases handled by circuit judges do not raise issues that are matters of first impression or otherwise legally consequential. In addition, as a general rule, these cases do not raise questions sufficiently salient to elicit much reaction from the judges deciding them. Based on their substantive content, some cases simply lack the content necessary to elicit dissensus in the form of dissents or reversals. Further, complex cases raising multifaceted issues requiring sophisticated analysis, and cases characterized by legal ambiguity for which the appropriate resolution is open to interpretation, can often result in disagreement simply because the law offers no straightforward or definitive outcome.

CHARACTERISTICS OF CIRCUITS. In addition to characteristics of judges and characteristics of cases, there are also characteristics of circuits (that is, institutional factors) that shape judicial behavior and, in particular, the expression of dissensus. Human institutions are those man-made organizational structures and rules that assist us in achieving our collective objectives by constraining and channeling human behaviors toward a particular end (see March and Olsen 1984). Law falls into this definition, as it constitutes a normative structure that shapes individual action. In addition to law, however, other institutional features are likely to influence judicial behavior. While clearly relevant to legislative outcomes (see, for example, Polsby 1968; Krehbiel 1992), the importance of institutional rules and structures has also been demonstrated in the judicial context (e.g., Cohen 2002).

One key institutional feature that structures the behavior of judges is circuit norms. In an early study of the Maryland Supreme Court, Robert Sickels (1965) demonstrated the impact of collegial norms on individual justices' behavior, particularly with respect to the choice to dissent. Such norms may also be affected by other institutional features such as court size. Where judges sit on a small court with only a few fellow judges, they may be more sensitive to offending their colleagues than judges who sit on a large court, where the number of judges makes it more difficult to develop or sustain personal relationships (but see Cohen 2002, 160–66).

The intermediate position of the U.S. Courts of Appeals within the federal judiciary imposes another institutionally based constraint on circuit judges. As noted earlier, unlike on the Supreme Court, appeals to the circuit courts are "as of right" in that circuit court judges generally must hear all appeals made to them. Though this is true in all circuits, its consequence in terms of workload is not uniform across circuits. Indeed, circuit judges' workloads vary substantially depending on the circuit in which they serve, with judges on some circuits shouldering a significantly greater caseload burden than others.[16] Such workload pressures may constrain judges who simply do not have the time, for example, to contemplate or articulate a dissenting opinion (cf. Howard 1981, 205).

Institutions can matter in yet another way. A venerable line of judicial scholarship has viewed judicial decision making from the perspective of small group theory (Pritchett 1948; Sickels 1965; Murphy 1966; Ulmer 1971; Atkins 1973; Walker 1973). In the case of the Supreme Court, with its stable membership, it is largely the *same* group of individuals who render decisions collectively time after time. The situation differs, however, on the U.S. Courts of Appeals in an important way. Decision making is the product of randomly selected three-judge panels.[17] Although a three-judge panel renders the initial circuit court ruling in almost all cases, a dissatisfied litigant may request reconsideration of the panel's ruling by the entire circuit *en banc.* To obtain *en banc* review, a litigant must formally submit a request for rehearing by the circuit *en banc* and secure consent from a majority of the circuit judges.[18] *En banc* review is rare, occurring in only a small percentage of cases (Solimine 1988; George and Solimine 2001). Yet circuit judges are surely cognizant that the full circuit can and might intervene to alter a decision made at the panel level, especially where the judge is dissatisfied with the panel's ruling (Van Winkle 1997). This unique institutional feature of the federal appeals courts, therefore, has the potential to shape judicial behavior—either by constraining judges from rendering decisions in accordance with their own preferences to avoid *en banc* review or by motivating judges to highlight discrepancies in the panel decision to generate *en banc* review.

Similar considerations regarding review by the Supreme Court may also come into play. That is, a judge on a three-judge panel unhappy with the majority opinion may calculate that the Supreme Court, if it were to review the decision, would issue a ruling more consistent with that judge's preferences. Alternatively, the judge may believe Supreme Court review will lead to an even less (from his perspective) desirable outcome than that represented by the majority opinion. In either case, a strategic judge may alter his behavior with regard to the expression of horizontal dissensus if he thinks that dissensus is more (or less) likely to trigger a favorable outcome.

In general, these considerations—which go well beyond the attitudinal model—extend our portrait of judges' actions and reflect the complexity of the decision-making environment within which judges on the U.S. Courts of Appeals work. In this book, we employ a more integrated theory based on the considerations outlined above to explain circuit judges' choices to write separate opinions and to reverse the trial court, each of which represents a form of dissensus (horizontal and vertical, respectively). We continue in the next section by applying these ideas to the choice to write a dissent or concurrence.

The Choice to Write a Separate Opinion

Drawing on the three major approaches to understanding judicial behavior discussed in the previous section, we develop an integrated model of separate opinion writing in this section. We take the theoretical arguments and empirical findings from previous research regarding the effects of judicial attitudes, judge characteristics, and circuit characteristics on various forms of judicial behavior and extend that scholarship to one particular form of judicial behavior, separate opinion writing.

ATTITUDINAL PREDICTORS OF SEPARATE OPINIONS. If attitudinal preferences manifest themselves in vote choice, judges whose ideological predilections place them in the minority may feel the need to express their disagreement by authoring a dissenting opinion. In other words, "[f]rom an attitudinal perspective, dissent is the product of ideological disagreement among the justices" (Brace and Hall 1993, 918).

Indeed, there is evidence to suggest that separate opinions (both concurrences and dissents) are, at least in part, a function of ideological disagreement between judges. At the Supreme Court, both Gregory Rathjen (1974) and Saul Brenner and Harold Spaeth (1988) found the ideological position of a justice relative to his brethren to be influential in prompting dissents.[19] More recently, Paul Wahlbeck and his colleagues (Wahlbeck, Spriggs, and Maltzman 1999) considered a justice's decision to author a separate opinion as a choice among four alternatives: to join the majority opinion, to write (or join) a regular concurrence, to write (or join) a special concurrence,[20] or to write (or join) a dissenting opinion. Their results provide strong evidence that separate opinions are a function of ideological disagreement among the justices. Even though Wahlbeck, James Spriggs, and Forrest Maltzman emphasize the strategic and institutional elements structuring the expression of such ideological disagreement, the bottom line is that ideological divergence among judges is an extremely influential determinant of separate opinions (see also Maltzman, Spriggs, and Wahlbeck 2000). In their research on state courts of last resort, Paul Brace and Melinda Gann Hall (1993) similarly focused on the strategic element of dissenting behavior, particularly vis-à-vis electoral considerations and institutional structures. Nonetheless, their analyses of individual judges' decisions to cast a dissenting vote in death penalty cases across six states demonstrate the importance of ideological considerations in those decisions. Clearly, then, existing research supports the conclusion that the attitudinal model has important implications for horizontal dissensus on appellate courts.

THE CONSEQUENCES OF INSTITUTIONAL ROLES. Virtually all institutions have memberships with at least some differentiation in roles. Those roles may be formally or informally defined, but they nonetheless influence behavior. In the case of the U.S. Courts of Appeals, there are several institutional roles that can lay claim (at least theoretically) to shaping the decision to author a separate opinion. As noted earlier, each circuit has a chief judge responsible for the administration of justice within the circuit. Given such a position of institutional authority, the chief may feel particularly responsible for ensuring collegial relations among judges in the circuit and, hence, be less likely to file dissenting opinions. In the case of concurring opinions, the relationship is likely to be slightly different. While dissents are direct expressions of attitudinal disagreement, concurrences, by their nature, are less about attitudinal disagreement as to appropriate outcomes and more about disagreement over the appropriate legal reasoning relied on to arrive at that outcome. Accordingly, chief judges may see concurrences as less threatening to collegial relations within a circuit than dissenting opinions and thus be more willing to suppress dissents than to suppress concurrences.

Similarly, freshman judges may be more inclined to defer to their senior brethren on the panel, though for different reasons. While chief judges are likely to do so because of their responsibilities for the administration of the circuit, freshman judges are likely to do so because of their uncertainty in their new roles. In addition, when district court judges sit by designation on appeals court panels, they may be more likely to defer to the more experienced and full-time circuit judges on the panel. As a result, district court judges sitting by designation may be less likely to dissent or concur when serving on the appeals court (Brudney and Ditslear 2001). Conversely, judges who have taken senior status, whereby they often enjoy a reduced caseload, have more of an opportunity to craft separate opinions if they so choose. Further, they may find themselves out of step with the views of the current majority on the circuit. Hence, senior judges have both the opportunity and (potentially) the motivation to file separate opinions more frequently.

THE EFFECT OF OTHER JUDGE CHARACTERISTICS. Institutional roles are not the only characteristics of judges that matter. Judicial behavior may also be influenced by the background characteristics of the individual judges on the panel. In terms of background, consider the fact that not all court of appeals jurists arrive at the bench after following the same career path. They differ in terms of their past professional experiences and qualifications. Many have served as federal judges in lower courts, giving them greater facility with federal case law. Still others have accumulated appellate experience on state court benches, giving them greater skill with appellate procedure. In either case, such judges come to the bench better equipped in terms of the skills necessary for crafting separate opinions. In addition, judges differ in their qualifications for the bench. For example, for more than four decades before the George W. Bush administration, nominees for the federal bench were rated by the American Bar Association (Grossman 1964). These ratings are based on judicial temperament, experience, character, and age (Carp and Stidham 1998, 227) and arguably provide some indication of a judge's reputation.

In considering the decision to author a separate opinion, reputation has the potential to shape the decisional calculus of a judge who is interested in safeguarding his good reputation. On the one hand, such a judge may see a separate opinion as a vehicle for further enhancing his reputation by giving him a forum for articulating his own ideas of the law. On the other hand, such a judge may be disinclined to author separate opinions, seeing them as potentially detrimental to his good reputation by marking him as difficult or injudicious.

THE INFLUENCE OF CASE CHARACTERISTICS. As noted earlier, not all cases are created equal, particularly in the U.S. Courts of Appeals. Given these courts' mandatory dockets, substantial variation exists across cases with respect to the cases' salience and their intrinsic interest to individual judges. Moreover, to the extent that a case is complex or the relevant rule of law ambiguous, the opportunities for disagreement multiply. Since filing a dissenting or concurring opinion requires a significant time commitment and presents a potential threat to collegial relations with the other two members of the panel, circuit judges likely choose their battles carefully and thus write separate opinions (dissents in particular) only in those cases where substantial disagreement exists or where the issue is of profound importance to the judge, society, and/or the development of the law. In short, salient, complex, and ambiguous cases all are more likely to foster the expression of dissensus among judges.

THE IMPACT OF INSTITUTIONAL NORMS AND STRUCTURES. Institutional factors shape dissenting and concurring behavior, too. The circuits differ across several dimensions. One such important variation is in norms across circuits. Informal norms are notoriously slippery and can be difficult to define, much less measure. One useful definition is that norms "are informal rules that specify certain behaviors as appropriate or inappropriate for individuals who occupy roles within a social institution" (Walker 1997, 2). Of course, measuring the psychology of shared attitudes regarding the permissible bounds of behavior requires sensitive survey instruments or interview protocols. Behavioral manifestations of norms can, however, serve as meaningful surrogates for the presumed underlying beliefs (Kirkpatrick and McLemore 1977). In the case of the expression of preferences in judicial decision making, different circuits have different norms regarding that expression. Judges on some circuits may be less tolerant of dissents because they believe that dissenting opinions undermine collegiality or create uncertainty in precedent. In such circuits, informal or unspoken norms may develop that reduce the likelihood of dissent (Sickels 1965). Such norms are likely to be a function of circuit size as well. Circuit size is a nontrivial consideration because it varies substantially. For example, the Court of Appeals for the First Circuit has a mere six authorized judgeships compared to the twenty-eight authorized judgeships in the sprawling Ninth Circuit. In small circuits where judges expect to serve on panels with their colleagues frequently, collegiality may be a more critical consideration. On large circuits, these concerns may be diminished simply because the judges have fewer interactions with each other.

Circuits also differ in terms of their workloads. Consider the number of appeals terminated on the merits. In 1996 the U.S. Courts of Appeals collectively disposed of over 27,000 appeals, but these appeals were not evenly distributed across circuits. While the D.C. Circuit disposed of just fewer than 700 appeals on the merits, the Ninth Circuit disposed of over 4,400 appeals. Moreover, although there is a relationship between the size of a circuit and the number of cases disposed of, it is not universally true that larger circuits handle more cases. For example, the Eleventh Circuit, with its twelve authorized judgeships, handled over 3,000 cases, more than four times that disposed of by the Tenth Circuit with the same number of authorized judgeships. Even more dramatically, the Eleventh Circuit's caseload exceeded by more than 1,000 cases the caseload in the Second, Third, Fourth, and Sixth Circuits even though each of these circuits had more authorized judgeships in 1996. Workload may matter because it is influential—if not determinative—of the time judges have to articulate disagreement with their peers.

STRATEGY AND THE DISSENTING OPINION. Finally, a judge's choice to author a separate opinion may have a strategic dimension, particularly in the case of dissent. If we assume that judges wish to embody their attitudinal preferences in federal law, a dissenting opinion may potentially serve as a useful tool to achieve that objective. To wit, at the U.S. Courts of Appeals, the *en banc* feature of the courts' institutional design and the U.S. Supreme

Court's authority to review circuit court decisions offer circuit judges the opportunity to use dissents strategically. First, circuit judges may choose to dissent to signal the circuit *en banc* that the majority panel opinion is contrary to circuit law or contrary to the preferences of the circuit majority. Steven Van Winkle's (1997) examination of search and seizure decisions at the U.S. Courts of Appeals offers some empirical evidence in support of this proposition. Of course, the *en banc* procedure could also lead to the suppression of dissenting opinions if a judge fears that an *en banc* decision would move the outcome even farther from the individual judge's preferred legal position than the panel's majority opinion. The extent to which appeals judges do, in fact, use separate opinions in such a fashion will depend on the configuration of preferences across the relevant actors: the judge, the three-judge panel, and the circuit as a whole.

Second, court of appeals judges may use dissent as a strategic tool to signal the Supreme Court and thereby invite review by that body. Analysis by Gregory Caldeira, John Wright, and Christopher Zorn (1999) demonstrates clearly that lower court dissent enhances the likelihood of Supreme Court review (see also Perry 1991). Presumably circuit court jurists are aware of this fact and could, if they so desired, attempt to use it to their advantage in much the same way as signaling the circuit *en banc*.

When it comes to horizontal dissensus, then, we expect that a variety of factors will influence circuit judges' choices to dissent or concur from the panel majority. Although we began with the attitudinal model of judicial decision making, we added other theoretical expectations regarding this critical aspect of judicial behavior. As was the case with horizontal dissensus, the attitudinal model serves as a useful starting point in thinking about vertical dissensus (manifested by the decision to reverse the lower court), but it can be profitably extended by considering differences in judges, cases, and circuits, as we outline below.

The Panel's Choice to Reverse

As in the previous section, we draw on the three major approaches to understanding judicial behavior discussed at the beginning of this chapter to develop an integrated model of separate opinion writing. We again take the theoretical arguments and empirical findings from previous research regarding the effects of judicial attitudes, judge characteristics, and circuit characteristics on various forms of judicial behavior, this time extending that scholarship to a second form of judicial behavior, appellate court reversal of a lower court decision.

ATTITUDINAL PREDICTORS OF REVERSAL. Circuit judges reverse district courts as part of error correction; that is, appellate review is the primary tool for identifying "error" and reversal is the primary tool for correcting "error." Yet, given the ambiguity in legal language, a judge's conception of legal error may well be structured by her attitudes or policy preferences. For that reason, a reasonable expectation is that a panel's decision to reverse a lower court will be conditioned by attitudinal factors.[21] In other words, "the outcome of appellate review may be expected to vary with the level of agreement between the preferences of the reviewing panel and the policy position taken by the trial judge" (Haire, Lindquist, and Songer 2003, 150).

Like judges on appellate panels, appellate and trial court judges may not necessarily share the same ideological preferences. To the extent that trial court judges render decisions that are driven, at least in part, by their policy preferences, situations may arise in which the outcome at the trial level deviates from the appellate court's preferred policy position. Such ideological differences may affect appellate judges' choices whether to affirm or reverse the lower court (Haire, Lindquist, and Songer 2003). Research on lower court compliance with the policy prescriptions of higher courts provides compelling evidence that, in general, ideological trends in decision making in the former track those in the latter (Baum 1980; Gruhl 1980; Songer and Sheehan 1990; Songer, Segal, and Cameron 1994; Benesh 2002). Of course, documented cases of willful disobedience on the part of lower courts are not unknown (e.g., Peltason 1961) and, in fact, such cases have motivated a number of studies on judicial compliance with high court precedents (e.g., Murphy 1959; Canon 1973, 1974). The key implication of the attitudinal model with regard to lower court reversal is that, as ideological differences between lower and higher courts increase, the greater the opportunity for ideological disagreement to arise and, hence, the greater the likelihood of reversal.

THE CONSEQUENCES OF INSTITUTIONAL ROLES. As with separate opinions, the institutional positions of judges on a decision-making panel have the potential to structure their propensity to reverse a lower court ruling under review. Those institutional roles that are likely to affect the decision to reverse, however, are somewhat different than those likely to affect separate opinion authorship. In this case, two institutional roles in particular have prima facie claims for influencing the decision to reverse: the chief judge and the district court judge sitting by designation.

Chief judges have the primary administrative responsibilities for their respective circuits (cf. Wasby 2003). Undoubtedly, reversals have at least the potential to compromise the smooth operation of a circuit for a variety of reasons, not the least of which is their potential to damage cordial relations between district and circuit court judges. When a chief judge authors majority opinions, he may thus be less inclined to reverse in order to maintain harmony between the trial and appellate judges within the circuit. Likewise, even when he does not serve as the majority opinion author, a chief judge may use his powers of persuasion to convince fellow panel members to affirm the lower court ruling in the interests of harmonious relations. However, concern for the smooth administration of a circuit could generate a tension between the goal of maintaining cordial relations, on the one hand, and "the concomitant desire to publicize 'corrected error' to all district courts in the circuit," on the other (Hettinger, Lindquist, and Martinek 2003b, 100). To the extent that reversals serve to ensure uniformity in the application of law throughout a circuit—and thereby enhance efficiency—a chief judge might well be more prone to influence panels of which he is a member to reverse.

Consider, too, a district court judge sitting by designation. Though a number of scholars have raised concerns about the effects of such judges on the deliberative process (e.g., Green and Atkins 1978) and on perceptions of legitimacy (e.g., Alexander 1965), the available empirical evidence as to their behavior is limited.[22] From a theoretical perspective, even when a designated district judge does not author the majority opinion, his mere presence on a panel might matter in the sense of fostering greater sensitivity to the lower court by all members of the panel.

THE INFLUENCE OF CASE CHARACTERISTICS. Cases on the courts of appeals' docket are a heterogeneous lot, varying across multiple dimensions. Three such dimensions are especially likely to manifest an influence on a panel's decision to reverse a district court judge's decision: salience, complexity, and the quality of the legal argument. Salience may come into play in two ways. First, salient cases are, by definition, the kind of cases judges are likely to consider carefully. The more salient the case, the more likely a judge is to expend scarce resources (both time and energy) on it and, hence, the greater the chance of finding error in the lower court decision, whether that "error" is ideological in nature or more about the appropriate application of a legal rule. Further, in salient cases, judges may set a lower bar in terms of how egregious an error must be before it warrants reversal. The relationship between complexity and the likelihood of reversal can also be thought of in terms of error correction.

Complexity imposes obstacles on even the most diligent district court judge. In such cases, "even a well-reasoned view of a trial judge will be displaced by the well-reasoned view of a panel of appellate judges" (Newman 1992, 630). Simply put, greater complexity means that district court judges have more opportunities to make mistakes in identifying or applying the relevant rule of law, mistakes a panel will be able to identify and correct.

As for the quality of the legal argument, there is significant variation in the quality of legal representation litigants are able to secure. Given the routine nature of much of the workload at the courts of appeals (Songer, Sheehan, and Haire 2000, 134), the presumption is in favor of affirming the lower court ruling (Songer, Sheehan, and Haire 2000, 105). Hence, an appellant seeking reversal is fighting an uphill battle and is unlikely to be successful in the absence of expert counsel with the ability to craft high-quality legal arguments to rebut that presumption of affirmance.

THE IMPACT OF INSTITUTIONAL NORMS AND STRUCTURES. As is the case with the decision to author a separate opinion by an individual circuit court judge, the decision by a circuit court panel to reverse a district court ruling is one that occurs within, and is likely to be shaped by, the institutional context. The more difficult it is for a district court judge to determine what the circuit will consider a correct ruling, the more likely it is for that judge to err and be reversed. The mixed signals sent by separate opinions make such errors more likely. While ambiguity has to do with the district court judge's side of the equation, there are other factors that are more related to the circuit side of the equation.

First, circuit norms may affect reversal decisions. In some circuits, norms may have arisen regarding the appropriate scope of the appellate court's reviewing authority, thus resulting in norms reflecting greater or lesser deference to the trial court. These norms are reflected in a circuit's prior propensity to reverse. Second, workload considerations—which tap into the notion of opportunity—are likely to arise. Reversing requires a greater time commitment than affirming; a reversal must be more carefully justified and directions must often be provided regarding procedures on remand. More fundamentally, finding and confirming error requires a careful review of the record and the parties' briefs, which is also time consuming. Reversal may simply be an option that is not exercised because of a lack of time and energy.

A Note about Data

To evaluate the propositions outlined above empirically, we rely on the U.S. Courts of Appeals Database (Songer 2002), which was funded by the National Science Foundation for use by scholars of judicial politics and behavior. It contains information on a random sample of appeals court cases from each circuit for each year for the 1925–96 period. This sample of cases was drawn from the universe of cases in which published opinions were issued.[23] Each case was coded for a variety of variables of interest to public law scholars, including basic case characteristics (e.g., the procedural history of the case, the date of the decision, the docket number), information concerning the litigants and other participants in the appeals process (e.g., the type of litigant, the number of litigants, the identity of intervenors), detailed information on the legal issues raised in each case (e.g., criminal, civil rights, privacy, labor relations, economic activity), and the identity of presiding judges and their votes.

The U.S. Courts of Appeals Database is commonly referred to as the Songer Database. Donald Songer, Reginald Sheehan, and Susan Haire (2000) are the first to use this database in any extensive way. They examine major trends in decision making on the U.S. Courts of Appeals, including changes in their agenda, the types of litigants coming before them, and the nature of issues adjudicated in those courts. Songer and his colleagues also offer information regarding trends in the incidence of separate opinions and lower court reversal, thereby providing an invaluable foundation for accounts of both the individual judge decision to author a separate opinion and the panel decision to reverse the lower court at the macro level. Ashlyn Kuersten and Songer (2001), too, provide useful information about the U.S. Courts of Appeals based on the Songer Database, along with practical information on the use of the Database (see also George and Sheehan 2000).

Conclusion

In this chapter, we have articulated a set of theoretical expectations regarding, first, the decision of an individual judge serving on the U.S. Courts of Appeals to author a separate opinion and, second, the decision of a three-judge panel of the U.S. Courts of Appeals to reverse a lower court ruling. We began with the well-established attitudinal model, the antecedents of which can be found in the legal realism of the early twentieth century and which currently dominates scholarly thinking regarding the behavior of judges. We were also mindful that, as powerful as the attitudinal model has proven to be as an explanation of behavior on the U.S. Supreme Court, the context of decision making on the U.S. Courts of Appeals makes it unlikely that attitudinal factors alone can account for circuit judges' observed behavior. In other words, rather than relying solely on the attitudinal model of behavior in the circuit courts, we elaborated on this foundation to consider characteristics of judges, characteristics of cases, and characteristics of circuits and their likely effects on both the decision to author a separate opinion—what we have labeled horizontal dissensus—and the decision to reverse a lower court—what we have labeled vertical dissensus. With these theoretical considerations in mind, we begin in the next chapter to evaluate these ideas empirically, starting with the choice of an individual judge to author a separate opinion.

THREE

Why Do Judges Write Separate Opinions?

In the previous chapter, we presented a theoretical portrait of judicial decision making, with particular attention given to factors that would affect horizontal or vertical dissensus on the federal appellate bench. In this chapter, we begin to put those theoretical ideas to an empirical test by specifying a model of horizontal dissensus that we evaluate using data from the U.S. Courts of Appeals Database (Songer 2002). Here, we focus on cases included in the Songer Database decided during the 1960 to 1996 period.[1] We also supplemented these data with a variety of additional information that we collected specifically for our purposes in exploring horizontal dissensus.

In this chapter, we are interested in explaining an individual judge's decision to file a separate dissenting or concurring opinion. Each observation in the Songer Database corresponds to a particular case. Among the information recorded for each observation is whether a separate opinion (concurring or dissenting) was filed. For the period under study, approximately 5.5 percent of the cases had concurring opinions, while about 9.5 percent of the cases had dissenting opinions. We examined each case identified as containing a separate opinion to determine which judge on each three-judge panel wrote the concurrence or dissent.[2] This information serves as the basis of a three-part dependent variable in the model of separate opinion authorship we explore in this chapter. For purposes of this analysis, we converted each case to three separate observations—one for each judge, and then restricted the analysis to the two judges who did not write the majority opinion. Thus, for each member of a three-judge panel who did not write the majority opinion, this trichotomous variable reflects whether the judge in question (1) filed a separate dissenting opinion, (2) filed a separate concurring opinion, or (3) joined the majority opinion. In terms of dissensus, both filing a dissenting opinion and filing a concurring opinion represent a manifestation of horizontal dissensus. Obviously, the latter is a milder version of horizontal dissensus than the former, but, in both cases, a court of appeals judge is formally and publicly articulating his disagreement with his peers on the decision-making panel. In the next section, we turn to developing an explanatory model to account for horizontal dissensus (as captured by that trichotomous dependent variable), a model that reflects the theoretical constructs discussed in chapter 2.

Specifying a Model of Separate Opinion Authorship

We now turn to developing an explanatory model to account for horizontal dissensus (as captured by the trichotomous dependent variable discussed above). The model we construct below further elaborates on the theoretical constructs discussed in chapter 2. In constructing our model, we pay close attention to appropriately translating these theoretical constructs into measurable variables with which to evaluate our theoretical expectations.

IDEOLOGY. Earlier, we noted the importance of attitudinal influences on decision making in appellate courts. Judges on the U.S. Courts of Appeals, like their counterparts on the U.S. Supreme Court, often decide cases in accordance with their personal policy preferences (see, for example, Howard 1981). The difference between the influence of attitudes in Supreme Court decision making and the influence of attitudes in courts of appeals decision making is a matter of degree rather than kind. The institutional environment of the Supreme Court simply imposes fewer constraints on the expression of attitudes than is true in the courts of appeals. Regardless of the institutional environment, however, and as Sheldon Goldman observed thirty-five years ago, "ideological differences are at the heart of dissensus" (1969, 218). In evaluating influences on dissensus, therefore, attitudinal explanations cannot be overlooked and must be accounted for.

In the context of a three-judge panel and horizontal dissensus, separate opinion authorship is likely to be structured by the degree of ideological diversity among the members of a decision-making panel. In general, when a panel discusses cases in conference following oral argument, individual panel members announce their position regarding whether the appellant should prevail. The senior member on the panel or the chief judge, if he is a member of the panel, assigns the majority opinion to himself or to another judge in the majority, who then crafts the opinion for the panel.[3] Subsequently, a panel member may announce his intent to dissent from the majority opinion or, alternatively, to concur with that opinion. Accordingly, the majority opinion writer has primary control over the content of the opinion, but he certainly will consider input from fellow panel members when the opinion is circulated.[4] In terms of ideological diversity, then, the important dynamic is the relationship between the majority opinion writer and each of the other two members of the panel. Hence, we hypothesize that the more divergent the policy preferences are between a judge and the majority opinion writer, the more likely that judge is to dissent (or at least not to concur). There is simply more room for disagreement regarding the appropriate resolution and/or legal basis for that resolution between two judges when they do not share the same ideological outlook.

Obviously, to evaluate this hypothesis empirically, we need some suitable measure of individual judge ideology. It is essential for any valid and reliable measure of the ideology of judges on the U.S. Courts of Appeals bench to take into account the means by which those judges are selected. As stipulated in the Constitution, the president nominates individuals to fill vacancies on the circuit court bench. Accordingly, one simple measure of judicial ideology is the political party affiliation of the judge's appointing president (e.g., Songer and Davis 1990; Songer and Haire 1992). Using the party of the appointing president is problematic in two regards, however. First, simple political party affiliation does not reflect the fact that there are significant variations in ideology even under the same party label. Simply put, "Eisenhower is not Reagan" (Giles, Hettinger, and Peppers 2002, 3). Thus, partisan affiliation is too crude a measure to adequately capture ideological preferences.

Party of the appointing president falls short as an adequate measure of judicial preferences in a second meaningful way. Though the president has the sole constitutional prerogative to nominate individuals to the federal bench (including the U.S. Courts of Appeals), individuals so nominated must be confirmed by a majority vote in the U.S. Senate. In other words, staffing the federal bench "represents one of the constitutionally mandated intersections of otherwise separate powers" (Martinek, Kemper, and Van Winkle 2002, 337). The literature on the appointment and confirmation process for lower federal court judges is voluminous to say the very least.[5] A persistent theme in this body of research is that the Senate is not merely a passive actor in the confirmation process. To be sure, some senators adopt the view that presidential choices should enjoy a presumption of confirmation. But, as Lauren Cohen Bell (2002b) documents, the history of confirmation politics evidences a decisive move away from deference to the president and a concomitant move to heightened scrutiny of nominees on the part of the Senate (see Hartley and Holmes 1997, 2002).

A key element of senatorial processing of lower federal court nominees is the norm (or tradition) of senatorial courtesy. "In its narrowest and most exact sense, 'senatorial courtesy' requires that the body of senators be guided in its action on a nomination by the attitudes of the senators from the state immediately affected by such nomination" (Cole 1937, 1113). Practically speaking, this norm means that presidents consult with senators who share their partisan affiliation and who represent the state in which the vacancy has arisen (see Goldman 1967). Given that district court borders are confined within a single state, the influence of senatorial courtesy is most pronounced when the nomination is to fill a district court judgeship (Chase 1972, 43–44; Sheldon and Maule 1997, 184). However, though each court of appeals includes within its boundary lines more than one state, there is still room for senatorial courtesy to matter because, by tradition, each state in the circuit has at least one seat on the circuit court. When a vacancy occurs, the senator from the particular state historically "assigned" to that seat is conventionally considered the "home-state" senator (see Carp, Stidham, and Manning 2004, 134). Using the voting behavior of circuit court judges appointed by Presidents Eisenhower through Reagan, Micheal Giles, Virginia Hettinger, and Todd Peppers (2001) demonstrate that, indeed, senatorial courtesy is a powerful force that moderates the influence of the president's preferences in the process of staffing the courts of appeals bench.

Accordingly, we need a measure of judge ideology that takes into account the influence of home-state senators in the selection of courts of appeals judges. Based on their previous research, Giles, Hettinger, and Peppers (2002) developed an ideology measure that is sensitive to that senatorial influence. They begin with work by Keith Poole (1998) that develops ideology scores for legislators and presidents; these scores are comparable across both chambers and branches as well as over time.[6]

In light of presidential prerogatives in the appointment process, Giles and his colleagues assign each judge appointed to the circuit bench in the absence of senatorial courtesy the Poole ideology score corresponding to his or her appointing president. However, for those judges appointed when there was one home-state senator of the president's party, Giles, Hettinger, and Peppers give those judges the Poole ideology score corresponding to that home-state senator. When both home-state senators were of the president's party, the corresponding ideology score for the judge is equal to the average Poole score of the two senators. The resulting measure of individual judge ideology has two desirable characteristics. First, unlike party of the appointing president, it is sensitive to variations in the ideological preferences of different presidents from within the same party. Second, it reflects the dynamic underlying judicial selection for the lower federal bench.

Drawing on this previous work, we used these scores to compare each (nonmajority opinion writing) judge on a three-judge panel to the majority opinion writer to determine the degree of ideological compatibility between the two.[7] To do so, we simply calculated the absolute value of the arithmetic distance between the score of the majority opinion writer and a (potential) separate opinion writer. This means that greater values on this variable indicate greater levels of ideological disagreement. The greater the ideological disagreement between the two, the more probable the expression of horizontal dissensus in the form of a dissenting or concurring opinion.

INSTITUTIONAL ROLES. In most regards, individuals serving on the U.S. Courts of Appeals are coequal with their peers. Though the U.S. Courts of Appeals are certainly part of a hierarchical judicial system, within that tier there is little to no formal differentiation in terms of power. Each circuit court judge is, in many important ways, an independent agent. Nonetheless, there are roles (both formal and informal) that are occupied by different judges within a circuit and that are potentially consequential in shaping the decision of a judge to file a dissenting or concurring opinion. Four such roles are particularly relevant here: chief judge, freshman judge, senior judge, and district court judge sitting by designation.

The chief circuit judge is the administrative head of the circuit (which includes the district courts located within the circuit) and has numerous statutory and organizational duties (see Wheeler and Nihan 1988; Hettinger, Lindquist, and Martinek 2003b; Wasby 2003). Among many other things, the chief judge (1) presides over the circuit judicial council, which is the body responsible for making "necessary and appropriate orders for the effective and expeditious administration of justice within its circuit,"[8] (2) is a member of the Judicial Conference, the central governing body for the entire federal court system, and (3) manages case flow and dispositions within his respective circuit. In addition to these administrative duties, the chief judge is also viewed as a general "problem solver" in the circuit (cf. Wheeler and Nihan 1988).

Chief judges have administrative responsibilities that are not trivial and can structure a chief's decision to author a separate opinion in two ways. First, as Russell Wheeler and Charles Nihan report, "[a]dministrative duties impose a very significant burden in time and energy upon appellate chief judges" (1988, 694). This is especially true because many chief judges take little or no caseload reduction from their usual duties as an appellate court judge (Wheeler and Nihan 1988, 695). This means that chief judges may simply be too busy to draft separate opinions. Second, by virtue of their administrative position—both the insight that position provides into the workings of the circuit and the responsibilities for smooth operations within the circuit it imposes—chief judges are likely to be more sensitive to issues of collegiality. To the extent chief judges are, in fact, sensitive about collegiality on their courts, they are likely to seek to reduce horizontal dissensus through self-restraint. In the sample of cases we use in this chapter, the chief appears as the potential dissenting or concurring judge almost 9 percent of the time, meaning there is more than ample opportunity to observe whether chief judges do behave differently from other, nonchief, judges and, as we expect, are less likely to author separate opinions.[9]

While the position of chief judge is a statutorily defined role with formal power and responsibilities, newly appointed judges also occupy an institutional role (albeit an informal one) that can structure separate opinion authorship. While chief judges have unique insights into the dynamics of their circuits, new judges are in a much different position. Since they are new to the court, new (or freshman) judges do not yet have substantial experience on the circuit to guide their behavior. Rather, new judges must acclimate themselves to their new environment (cf. Wasby 1989). In this regard, judges new to the U.S. Courts of Appeals are in much the same position as newly elected members of Congress (cf. Stratmann 2000). During this acclimation period, freshman judges learn about their colleagues and familiarize themselves with court norms, procedures, and expectations.[10] In short, "new judges come to the bench with less than perfect information as to how best to perform their responsibilities" (Hettinger, Lindquist, and Martinek 2003a, 793) and, thus, must spend some time to acquire the requisite information.

This is directly relevant for the decision to file a separate opinion for two reasons. First, freshman judges may be less inclined to author a separate opinion, because they are simply unsure about the appropriate circumstances in which such opinions are warranted. Second, freshmen may be more hesitant to challenge senior colleagues by dissenting or concurring from majority opinions. To account for any "freshman effect," we include in our model of the decision to file a dissent or concurrence a measure indicating whether a potential separate opinion author is a freshman or not. Problematically, there is no definitive consensus as to what period of time reasonably constitutes a judge's acclimation or freshman period. For example, students studying acclimation effects at the Supreme Court have used, variously, the first term of service (Bowen and Scheb 1993), the first two terms of service (Hagle 1993), and the first four terms of service (Pacelle and Pauly 1996). In the limited research on this question at the U.S. Courts of Appeals, J. Woodford Howard suggested the period of adjustment would be a single year. However, in our previous work (devoted solely to the freshman effect for circuit court judges), we have found two years to be a reasonable measure, and that is the measure we use here (Hettinger, Lindquist, and Martinek 2003a). Such judges constitute over 11 percent of the observations in our sample. As in the case of the chief judge, our expectation is that a freshman judge will be less likely to author a separate opinion; that is, freshman judges will be less likely to engage in horizontal dissensus.[11]

Though freshman judges are, by definition, inexperienced judges in some potentially very important ways, senior judges are, by definition, "very experienced members of the court. With their accumulated insight and wisdom, they are a valuable national resource" (Feinberg 1990, 412). Judges who meet certain age and length-of-service requirements can, if they so desire, take senior status. Currently, judges sixty-five years or older, with fifteen years of experience, have the option of doing so. For each additional year of age, judges may take senior status with one less year of service. So, for example, a judge who is sixty-six years of age, with fourteen years of service, can take senior status, as can a judge who is sixty-seven years of age, with thirteen years of service. Senior judges continue to receive their full salaries and have access to both office staff and administrative support, but they have the option of hearing fewer cases. When a circuit court judge takes senior status, her position is officially considered vacant and available for presidential nomination and senatorial approval. Judges on senior status can serve to relieve the pressures of increasing caseloads and are now considered essential for the operation of the U.S. Courts of Appeals (Watson 1989; Van Duch 1996), especially in light of the persistent vacancies on the lower appellate bench (Citizens for Independent Courts 2000).

Notwithstanding their contributions in this regard, senior-status judges also have the potential to affect the incidence of horizontal dissensus. This is so for reasons related both to opportunity and motive. First, with regard to opportunity, senior judges often have a comparative luxury of time not enjoyed by regular active-duty judges, time that can be devoted to crafting dissenting and concurring opinions. Second, with regard to motivation, senior judges may be "less representative of the consensus of the court than those of the active judges" (Carrington 1969, 563). Further, such judges may be more sensitive to the judicial legacy they are likely to leave. The existing evidence on this point is very limited and circumscribed at best (cf. Higgins and Rubin 1980). But, since such judges are not by any means rare participants in three-judge panel decision making (constituting, for example, over 15 percent of the cases in our sample), empirically assessing whether they do behave differently from active-duty judges is important. Our expectation in this regard is that such judges will be more likely to author a dissenting or concurring opinion.[12]

In contrast with judges on senior status, district court judges sitting by designation are apt to be less likely to pierce the fabric of collegiality by authoring separate opinions. Under 28 U.S.C. § 292, a judge may be designated to participate on appellate panels. Designation in this manner is the prerogative of the chief judge. Though there is some evidence to suggest that this practice is, in part, intended to provide a socialization experience for newly appointed district court judges (Wasby 1980–81), Richard Saphire and Michael Solimine found that circuit practices strongly suggested the use of designated district court judges was really more intended to address heavy workloads (1995, 362). Though the practice is not one that receives much attention outside of legal circles, it is quite common, with district court judges sitting by designation, by one estimate, in approximately one out of every five appellate panels in the federal courts (Brudney and Ditslear 2001, 565).

The regular participation of such judges has raised questions regarding their effects on the decision-making process on the U.S. Courts of Appeals. Empirical studies have demonstrated that the behavior of such judges does differ in meaningful ways from their appeals court colleagues on the same panels (Brudney and Ditslear 2001). James Brudney and Corey Ditslear draw the following conclusions about designated district court judges from their study of labor decisions in the U.S. Courts of Appeals: "As panel participants, district judges were markedly less assertive than their appellate colleagues. They did not vote distinctively for or against unions when compared with appellate counterparts. They also were less likely to author signed majority opinions or to issue dissents" (2001, 597).

In short, district court judges are not entirely fungible with courts of appeals judges. While Brudney and Ditslear's evidence is compelling, it is circumscribed by their substantive focus on labor decisions. Our interest here is to determine whether designated judges differ in their separate opinion authorship behavior in general. Do district court judges sitting by designation defer to their circuit court peers? In the sample of cases we analyze, such judges compose almost 9 percent of the cases. Our expectation is that they will be less likely to concur or dissent from the majority opinion.[13]

To summarize our hypotheses about institutional roles and the decision of a judge to file a dissent or concurrence, we expect judges occupying three of the four institutional roles we have identified (chief judge, freshman judge, designated district court judge) to be less likely to engage in horizontal dissensus. As for chief judges, the rationale for expecting such behavioral differences hinges on the administrative role the chief judge plays and his heavy responsibilities with regard to the smooth operation of the judicial machinery in his circuit. Simply put, chief judges are more likely to be concerned that separate opinions have the potential to fray collegial relations within the circuit. Freshman and designated district court judges, however, are less likely to file separate opinions because of their unfamiliarity with the work of a circuit court judge and deference to senior colleagues, in the former case, and superiors in the judicial hierarchy, in the latter case. With regard to judges who have taken senior status, however, our expectation is that they will be more likely to author separate opinions because they have both the opportunity and motive to do so.

JUDICIAL EXPERIENCE. Judges rendering decisions in the U.S. Courts of Appeals differ not only in terms of the institutional roles they do (or do not) occupy. They differ, too, with regard to their prior experiences. Such differences in prior experiences can be thought of as the socialization process judges undergo before ascending to the circuit court bench. Socialization, defined as education in the broadest sense, has often been linked to political behavior (Dawson, Prewitt, and Dawson 1977). While initial work on political socialization focused on childhood and adolescent experiences, later studies also focused on adult socialization as well (Niemi and Sobieszek 1977). In the area of judicial behavior, a small socialization literature exists addressing postappointment learning processes, including the study of freshman judges as noted above (see, for example, Carp and Wheeler 1972).

Preappointment experiences may also shape circuit judges' behavior, especially with regard to separate opinion authorship. Consider, for example, a judge who ascends to the U.S. Courts of Appeals after having served as a federal district court judge. Such a judge is already familiar with the work of courts of appeals judges in two ways. First, she is already familiar with the substance of the laws at issue in the cases before the bench because she dealt with the same body of federal law as a federal district court judge. Second, as a consequence of sitting by designation on circuit court panels, such a judge may come to the circuit court bench with a degree of familiarity regarding the norms governing separate opinions. These two factors suggest that an appellate court judge with prior service as a district court judge might well be less reticent to engage in horizontal dissensus. Judges who come to the U.S. Courts of Appeals differ in terms of yet another kind of experience. In particular, some judges have had the benefit of previously serving on another appellate court—almost invariably a state supreme court—and, therefore, enjoy a greater level of familiarity with appellate procedures and processes. If prior experience as a federal court judge breeds familiarity with the substance of federal law, prior experience as an appellate court judge breeds familiarity with the appellate process. In both cases, such familiarity can serve to mitigate any hesitancy to author separate opinions.[14]

JUDICIAL PRESTIGE. A final characteristic of judges that merits consideration as a candidate for structuring the decision to author a separate opinion is prestige. David Klein and Darby Morrisroe (1999) have persuasively demonstrated that an individual circuit judge's prestige or reputation in terms of citation frequency affects the likelihood that the judge's pronouncements will be adopted in other circuits. According to Klein and Morrisroe, judges may look to the reputation of other judges who have authored existing precedent as cues to help them answer difficult legal questions. In considering whether to apply such precedent, individual judges may give respected judges' opinions more credence, either because "respected judges' opinions display particular insight, logic, craftsmanship, or some other similar quality" or because they are moved "by their reputations alone" (373). From the perspective of a prestigious judge, concerns about husbanding his authority and using his good reputation to the best effect may lead such a judge to author fewer separate opinions.

Conversely, judges who enjoy prestigious reputations may be more comfortable writing separate opinions because they have more confidence about their colleagues' reactions thereto. In short, there are good reasons to suspect that judicial prestige could cut either way, making separate opinion authorship more or less likely.

Before we can untangle the relationship between prestige and separate opinion authorship, we must first identify a suitable measure of judicial prestige. Perhaps the most desirable such measure would be one based on comprehensive surveys of courts of appeals judges, in which judges were evaluated by their peers. Such a measure is difficult to come by, however. We have chosen to use American Bar Association (ABA) ratings of nominees to the federal bench to differentiate among judges based on their qualifications and reputations. For the years included in our study, the ABA regularly rated judges in terms of their judicial temperament, experience as a judge or law professor, age, and educational qualifications (Grossman 1964; Goldman 1997). These criteria were used to rate judges as exceptionally well qualified, well qualified, qualified, or unqualified. The rating of exceptionally well qualified was eliminated in 1991, so that the rating evolved to include only three categories.

Here, we use the ABA ratings to construct a dichotomous measure that distinguishes well-qualified or exceptionally well-qualified judges, on the one hand, from those receiving merely qualified or unqualified ratings, on the other hand. In the sample of cases we analyze here, 63 percent of the judges were rated as well qualified or above, while 37 percent were rated as qualified or below. As noted above, we have no directional hypothesis to offer with respect to this variable; that is, it may result in an enhanced *or* a diminished likelihood of separate opinion authorship. Though we do not offer a directional hypothesis with regard to the direction of the relationship, we do expect it to manifest some discernible effect.[15]

CASE FACTORS. Ideological disagreement between a judge and a majority opinion author, institutional roles, and the characteristics of individual judges are all important factors to consider when constructing an integrated model of the decision to dissent or concur. So, too, are characteristics that vary across cases. The fact of the matter is that all appellate cases are not created equal. Because the U.S. Courts of Appeals hear appeals as of right—that is, they have mandatory jurisdictions—much of their caseload consists of cases involving legal matters that are at least somewhat settled and thus do not raise issues that are likely to divide judges on the reviewing panel. Nevertheless, the courts of appeals are not strangers to cases dealing with highly controversial matters. Neither are they strangers to cases that are complex in nature or marked by ambiguity. Case salience, case complexity, and legal ambiguity are all characteristics likely to increase the likelihood of a separate opinion, though for different reasons.

Consider, first, the effect of case salience. Salient cases are more likely to result in separate opinions for a very straightforward reason: judges will be more likely to divert their scarce time and energy to producing separate opinions when a case is a salient one. Any number of factors could arguably serve as reasonable surrogates for the underlying concept of salience. Two readily come to mind: participation by amicus curiae and the presence of civil rights and civil liberties claims. A third party may participate in an appeal by filing an amicus curiae brief. Formally intended as a vehicle for providing additional information to judges to aid them in their decision making, amicus curiae briefs, with few exceptions, are filed by interest groups and are clearly intended to advocate for a particular resolution (Barker 1967). At the Supreme Court level, amicus curiae participation is almost de rigueur (Epstein 1991; cf. Collins 2004). This is not true, however, at the courts of appeals level, where amicus briefs emerge in only slightly more than 4 percent of the cases in the data we analyze here. This is not remarkable, since amicus brief preparation is expensive. The very infrequency of amicus curiae participation in the circuit courts, however, makes it a particularly apt measure of salience. Given that groups rarely participate in this way at the U.S. Courts of Appeals, the decision to do so is likely to reflect the importance of the case to the broader political and social community.[16]

Amicus participation is not the only viable measure of salience. Judges are human and, as such, are also more prone to pay close attention to a case that is of special interest to them. Cases involving a civil rights or civil liberties issue have a prima facie claim on being the kinds of cases circuit court judges will view as salient. Civil rights and civil liberties claims have to do with issues such as freedom of speech and religion, voting rights violations, and privacy rights. These cases constitute only a minority of the courts of appeals docket, on average less than 16 percent, although there is a nontrivial amount of variation across circuits, with the Tenth Circuit averaging less than 8 percent and the Eleventh Circuit averaging approximately 23 percent during the 1925-to-1988 period (Songer, Sheehan, and Haire 2000, 64, table 3.7). Despite their relative rarity, cases involving civil rights or liberties claims are most likely to capture the attention of appeals court judges and, hence, are the kinds of cases that are likely to prompt judges to author separate opinions.[17]

The complexity of a case is also likely to enhance the prospects of a separate opinion. In complex cases, more opportunities exist for judges to part company as to the appropriate resolution and/or legal rationale. As with case salience, more than one reasonable measure of case complexity exists. The presence of cross appeals and the number of issues raised are two likely candidates. In textbook descriptions of the appellate process, the litigant unhappy with the trial court result files an appeal, making her the appellant, while the litigant satisfied with the trial court decision becomes the appellee (or respondent). In real life, it is possible that neither litigant will be fully satisfied with the ruling of the district court. One party may be perfectly happy with the trial court's resolution of issues A and B but terribly unhappy with the trial court's resolution of issue C. The other party, however, may be thrilled with the outcome as to issue C and less than elated with the outcome as to issues A and B. In such a scenario, both may appeal the lower court decision. In our sample of cases, 6 percent entailed such cross appeals. Their presence indicates that the case has multiple dimensions and, almost by definition, is more likely to be complex. Accordingly, the case provides fertile ground for disagreement, potentially leading to separate opinion authorship.

The number of legal issues raised by the litigants also contributes to case complexity. When a panel must resolve a multitude of issues in a case, each separate issue offers another potential point of disagreement among panel members. All things being equal, the greater the number of issues raised, the more likely it is that the case itself is complex.

Where cases involve cross appeals or raise multiple issues, judges have more grounds on which to disagree. This suggests that the relationship between complexity and separate opinions may therefore simply be a matter of alternative outcomes; where multiple issues or appeals are presented, judges have greater choice concerning reasoning and case disposition.[18] In either case, separate opinion authorship is likely to be more frequent.

This is also likely to be true when a case evidences ambiguity as to its appropriate resolution. Arguably, reversal of the lower court reflects legal ambiguity because it represents a situation in which presumably reasonable federal judges, considering the same case, have come to different conclusions as to its appropriate resolution. This is not a trivial consideration, because lower court reversal is not rare. For example, almost 30 percent of the cases in our database involved a reversal of the lower court, in whole or in part. And, in fact, in prior studies of appellate court decision making, reversal (vertical dissensus) has been closely linked to dissenting behavior (horizontal dissensus). For example, in their early study of three circuit courts, Richard Richardson and Kenneth Vines found that there was three to six times as much conflict among panel members when the court of appeals reversed the district court than when it affirmed (1970, 135–36). This finding has been interpreted as reflecting the presence of "meaningful choice points," in that cases involving reversal often raise issues where the appropriate outcome is far from clear (Lamb 1986, 183).

Indeed, in his study of appellate reversals in the Second Circuit, Judge Jon Newman concluded that the "overwhelming proportion of reversals arose from disagreements between the Second Circuit and the district court on a reasonably debatable point of law" (1992, 638). Based on existing studies, we hypothesize that when the circuit panel reverses, the case likely involves an indeterminate legal question or matter of ambiguous textual interpretation. What divides the circuit court from the district court is also likely to divide the circuit judges from each other, thus resulting in horizontal dissensus.[19]

CIRCUIT CHARACTERISTICS. Having considered characteristics of judges and cases, our discussion now turns to factors related to characteristics of circuits. The influence of institutional factors in structuring decision making has been well established in a variety of contexts, including in judicial decision making (e.g., Brace and Hall 1993; Cohen 2002; Hall and Brace 1989; Langer 2002; Rohde 1972). In the discussion below, we distinguish between characteristics of circuits that structure the motivation and the opportunity to file separate opinions.

Let us consider motivation first. In some circuits dissensus may be viewed less favorably because norms have developed that promote consensus rather than dissensus. Other circuits may be more accepting of the expression of dissensus through separate opinions. Accordingly, we expect judges' behavior to vary in relation to circuit-level norms regarding dissenting or concurring opinions. While norms are difficult to measure, one reasonable way to do so is to use the behavioral manifestation of those norms as a surrogate. In this case, that means considering the prevalence of separate opinion authorship in a circuit in the previous year as a measure of norms regarding the acceptability of separate opinion authorship.[20]

Another, albeit more indirect, way of measuring norms of consensus is related to the size of a circuit. Certainly, in smaller circuits, one might expect that judges will be more sensitive to the possibility of offending their colleagues on the bench, with whom they will more frequently sit on three-judge panels. A useful analogy might be to think of the differences in norms of behavior in large lecture classes versus the norms of behavior in small seminar classes. Behavior that might be acceptable (if undesirable) in the former—for example, arriving late, chatting with classmates— would be unacceptable in small seminars, where students come to know one another and their professor on a more individual basis. Though the college classroom setting is far different from the setting within which judges on the U.S. Courts of Appeals operate, the logic is the same. One way to evaluate empirically the validity of this hypothesis is to take into account the size of the circuit. Accordingly, we include a measure representing the number of authorized judgeships per circuit per year.[21]

With regard to opportunity, we can think of judges' caseloads as determining the opportunity costs associated with separate opinion authorship. Caseload burdens vary widely across the circuit courts. Judges working in circuits with higher caseloads may not have the same time to devote to separate opinion authorship.[22] In the model of separate opinion authorship we offer here, we account for this possibility by including a measure of workload.[23]

Estimating a Model of Separate Opinion Authorship

Having developed a comprehensive explanation of an individual judge's decision to file a concurring or dissenting opinion, we now test this theoretically motivated explanation using empirical data. As noted earlier, much of the data come from the Songer Database and include a sample of cases from every circuit for every year from 1960 to 1996. The choice set facing a judge consists of three discrete choices: join the majority opinion, concur, or dissent. Each observation in the dataset represents one of those discrete choices in each case by each judge who is not the majority opinion writer. Thus, each individual court of appeals decision can generate up to two observations. This results in over 17,000 observations over the thirty-seven-year period. Concurrences are present in just over 3 percent of these observations and dissents are present in nearly 5 percent of these observations.[24]

Individual circuits and individual judges display different levels of separate opinion writing. In the twelve circuits over the thirty-seven-year period, 15 percent of the observations in the Third and Fourth Circuits included dissents in 1980. In contrast, we observed concurrences in each of three years in the Sixth Circuit that amounted to over 10 percent of the observations in each of those years. Of course, because of the relatively rare nature of concurrences and dissents, the dataset reports many circuits in many years with no concurrences or dissents. Of the 994 judges in the dataset, quite a few judges appear to dissent or concur in at least 50 percent of the cases in which they participate. Many of these judges, however, participated in a trivial number of cases. Among judges who participated in a nontrivial number of cases (ten or more), the percentage of dissents ranged as high as 27 percent, and the percentage of concurrences ranged as high as 22 percent.

One way of thinking about the set of options facing a judge is to consider them as a set of ordered choices: join majority > concur > dissent. Assuming that the choices are ordered in that fashion is problematic, however, because it assumes that a judge would prefer to register his disagreements with the majority opinion via a concurrence instead of a dissent, if possible. This assumption is not necessarily appropriate, however, given that differences between concurrences and dissents are often differences in kind rather than differences in degree. That is, concurrences are not simply "half" a dissent or "mini" dissents; dissents and concurrences represent qualitatively different perspectives for the authoring judge and thus cannot be neatly placed on a single continuum. A better option, then, is to consider them as an unordered set of alternatives from which a judge selects. This is what we do here with the use of an estimation technique called multinomial logit (MNL),[25] which allows us to evaluate whether the relationships we have hypothesized are supported empirically.[26]

It is not necessary to understand either the statistical theory underlying the MNL model or the mechanics of its estimation to gain an intuitive sense of what the results of the model tell us regarding the relationships we hypothesized. For interested readers, the full statistical results of the MNL estimation appear in the appendix to this chapter, along with descriptive statistics for all of the variables. Below, we use the statistical results we obtain from the MNL model to calculate the likelihood that a judge will file a concurrence or a dissent relative to the likelihood of simply joining the majority opinion.

As a preliminary point, it is important to note first that the statistical results suggest a similar but not identical dynamic underlying the decision to dissent compared to the dynamic underlying the decision to concur. Certain independent variables are helpful predictors of both types of separate opinion writing behavior, concurrences and dissents. Other variables, conversely, were useful in predicting concurrences but not dissents or vice versa. Table 1 summarizes the estimation results, indicating which variables did, in fact, manifest an influence and the direction of the substantive effect.

TABLE 1. Summary of separate opinion model

	CONCUR VERSUS JOIN THE MAJORITY	DISSENT VERSUS JOIN THE MAJORITY
Ideology		
Ideological disagreement	Concurrence *more* likely	Dissent *more* likely
Institutional roles		
Chief judge	No effect	Dissent *less* likely
Freshman judge	No effect	Dissent *less* likely
Designated district court judge	No effect	Dissent *less* likely
Senior judge	No effect	No effect
Judge characteristics		
Prior federal court experience	No effect	No effect
Prior appellate court experience	Concurrence *more* likely	No effect
ABA rating	No effect	Dissent *less* likely
Case factors		
Amicus curiae participation	Concurrence *more* likely	Dissent *more* likely
Civil rights/liberties claim	Concurrence *more* likely	Dissent *more* likely
Cross appeals	No effect	No effect
Number of issues raised	Concurrence *more* likely	No effect
Lower court reversal	Concurrence *more* likely	Dissent *more* likely
Circuit characteristics		
Separate opinion rate	Concurrence *more* likely	Dissent *more* likely
Size	No effect	No effect
Caseload	No effect	No effect

As table 1 indicates, ideological differences between a judge and the majority opinion writer matter, increasing the likelihood of observing both a concurrence and a dissent. Although this result is not surprising with respect to dissenting opinions—where judges disagree as to the fundamental outcome of the case—it is somewhat more interesting with respect to concurrences. In the case of a concurring opinion, the concurring judge agrees with the result reached by the majority but disagrees as to its rationale. Since ideology matters even in the case of concurring opinions, this result suggests the importance of ideology both to the directionality of the outcome (that is, whether a particular party wins) and to the legal justification regardless of result. In other words, ideology matters in more ways than one. For scholars of judicial politics, who traditionally have focused on the "ideological direction" of case outcomes as the critical dependent variable of interest, these findings indicate that a broader assessment of ideology, which includes opinion content as well as case outcome, is warranted. With regard to dissensus, these findings underscore the importance of ideology as an explanation for horizontal dissensus.

Other variables related to both concurrences and dissents include case salience, legal ambiguity, and norms regarding the acceptability of separate opinions. When judges weigh the opportunity costs associated with the drafting of separate opinions, case salience—indicated by amicus participation and/or the presence of a civil rights or civil liberties claim—is clearly an important element of that calculation. No doubt, judges consider the broader doctrinal or societal impact of cases when deciding whether to write separately, with more routine or mundane cases less likely to justify the time expenditure. Furthermore, case ambiguity, as reflected by reversal of the lower court, is also related to fragmented opinions and voting behavior within panels, both in terms of concurrences and dissents. At bottom, this result reflects the common sense idea that where the law is ambiguous, disagreement is more likely to arise, whether as to the case outcome or as to the majority's analysis. And finally, circuit level norms regarding separate opinion authorship are related to both dissenting and concurring opinions. When judges view dissents and concurrences as more commonplace, they apparently feel less reluctant to write such opinions themselves.

Equally interesting are those variables that help predict the occurrence of a dissent or a concurrence, but not both. First, variables related to institutional roles are good predictors of dissenting opinions but not of concurring opinions. Chief judges, freshman judges, and designated district court judges are all significantly less likely to dissent from the panel majority than are other judges. Their roles are not, however, related in any meaningful way to the likelihood of a concurrence. The fact that institutional role is related to dissenting rather than concurring opinions suggests that the key underlying dynamic may be related to collegiality concerns rather than to opportunity costs and time pressures. Although chiefs, freshman judges, and designated district court judges may be more pressed for time than other judges (because of administrative obligations, inexperience, and trial commitments, respectively), they are no less likely to author concurring opinions than others of their brethren. Conversely, they are less likely to author separate opinions that directly challenge the case outcome preferred by the panel majority.

In addition, judges with prior appellate experience are more likely to write concurring opinions, but no more or less likely to write dissenting opinions than their circuit court brethren. This finding may result from such judges' willingness to express or explore alternative methods to resolve case outcomes because they have more experience shaping opinions on another appellate court. Conversely, judges who have received the ABA's highest qualification ratings are significantly less likely to write a dissenting opinion. One of the ABA's assessment criteria involves "judicial temperament." Perhaps more-qualified judges are, indeed, more "tempered" in their approach to other panel members and thus less inclined to dissent.

Table 1 and our discussion so far have focused simply on which factors matter and whether they make concurrences and/or dissents more or less likely. Table 2 offers a different perspective on the meaning of our statistical results in substantive terms. Based on the full estimation results (reported in the appendix to this chapter), table 2 presents a variety of predicted probabilities associated with each of the statistically significant variables. The first row of the table shows the baseline predicted probabilities of joining the majority opinion, publishing a concurrence, or publishing a dissent. These baseline probabilities are computed by holding all continuous variables (such as the difference in ideology and the size of the circuit) at their mean values, while holding all discrete variables (such as chief and designated judge) at their modal values. The resulting probabilities are the equivalent of the average probability of observing each outcome (join majority, concur, dissent) and provide a useful starting point for evaluating the magnitude of the influence of each variable. As reported in table 2, the likelihood of publishing any kind of separate opinion is quite low, totaling less than 6 percent. The probability of a dissent is almost twice that of a concurrence.

The remaining rows in table 2 report the predicted probabilities for each outcome as we allow each statistically significant variable to take on different values, while holding all of the other variables constant at their respective baseline values.

Consider first the ideological difference between a potential separate opinion writer and the majority opinion author. As noted above, this variable matters both in terms of predicting concurrences and dissents. Comparing the baseline predicted probabilities of observing, respectively, a concurrence and a dissent when ideological difference is at its maximum observed value (that is, the maximum difference we see in our sample) gives us a sense of the substantive effects of ideological difference. The difference in absolute terms is rather small, with slightly less than a 0.01 increase in the probability of a concurrence and a 0.02 increase in the probability of a dissent. This means for both concurrences and dissents, the probability increases approximately 50 percent over the baseline. The fact that these changes are small in absolute terms is not at all surprising, given

TABLE 2. Predicted probabilities for separate opinions

	PROBABILITY OF MAJORITY	PROBABILITY OF CONCURRENCE	PROBABILITY OF DISSENT
Baseline	0.943	0.020	0.038
Maximum of ideological difference (1.158)	0.913	0.029	0.058
Minimum of ideological difference (0)	0.953	0.016	0.031
Chief judge	0.958	n.s.	0.024
Judge in first two years of appointment	0.956	n.s.	0.029
District judge sitting by designation	0.968	n.s.	0.016
Appellate court experience	0.940	0.031	n.s.
ABA qualified or lower	0.934	n.s.	0.048
Amicus brief filed	0.905	0.039	0.056
Civil rights or liberties issue	0.923	0.025	0.053
Maximum of issues listed in headnotes (7)	0.900	0.058	n.s.
Minimum of issues listed in headnotes (0)	0.950	0.014	n.s.
Opinion reverses lower court	0.921	0.025	0.054
Maximum rate of separate opinions (0.409)	0.775	0.092	0.133
Minimum rate of separate opinions (0.019)	0.969	0.010	0.022

that the likelihood of a concurrence or dissent is quite small to begin with. When we consider the effects in terms of percentage change, however, the effects are quite substantial.

Although none of the institutional role variables reach significance in the concurrence model, status as a chief judge or freshman judge have similarly sized negative effects on the probability of a dissent, reducing the respective probabilities by 0.015 and 0.009. The institutional role variable that exhibits the greatest negative effect on the probability of a dissent is the variable reflecting status as a designated district court judge. A district court judge sitting by designation is less than half as likely as a circuit court judge to write a dissenting opinion.

The case characteristic variable with the greatest effect on the probability of a separate opinion is the presence of an amicus brief. Cases that demonstrate sufficient legal or political importance for third parties to absorb the costs of filing a brief result in more dissents and concurrences. A concurrence is nearly twice as likely in these cases as in cases without amicus briefs, while a dissent is almost 50 percent more likely.

The single variable that has the widest effect over its entire range of values is the variable measuring circuit norms, which demonstrates the important influence of such norms on individual judge behavior. Over the entire range of observed separate opinion behavior (that is, the maximum to minimum rate of separate opinion writing we see in our data), the probability of joining the majority opinion ranges from 0.80 to 0.97. In circuits with the highest level of separate opinion writing, an individual judge is nearly two and a half times as likely to publish a concurrence or dissent as compared to the baseline. Clearly, norms within a circuit do shape behavior.

In our discussion of substantive results so far, we have isolated the effect of a single variable. In what follows, we allow several variables to take on hypothetical but realistic values to help illustrate the range of the likelihood of a dissent or concurrence. We compute predicted probabilities associated with the different combinations of values on the explanatory variables and show that, while the baseline probabilities of dissents or concurrences are quite low, under some very realistic circumstances, those probabilities can vary dramatically.

In the first example, we create a hypothetical judge in a hypothetical case by setting all of the variables that obtained statistical significance in the dissent model at values that would raise the probability of a dissent. To do so, we first identified a circuit with a high rate of separate opinion writing in the previous year and at least one panel in which the ideological distance between the judge and the majority opinion writer is also substantial. In this example, those values come from the D.C. Circuit in 1966. The highest rate of separate opinions appeared in the D.C. Circuit in 1965, when almost 41 percent of the cases contained a dissent and/or concurrence. Since chief judges, designated district court judges, and freshman judges are all *less* likely to issue a separate opinion, in this example we assume that the judge in this case has none of those characteristics. Our hypothetical judge is therefore a regularly serving court of appeals judge who has been on the court for at least two years. A judge who receives a well qualified rating is also less likely to dissent; therefore, we assume that this judge received a rating of qualified or lower. We also set the ideological distance between our hypothetical judge and the majority opinion writer at a value of 0.701, which is nearly twice the average but less than half the maximum amount observed in our sample.

We further assume that the case involves an issue of civil rights or civil liberties, that a third party filed an amicus brief, and that the majority decision reverses the lower court. The variables that are nonsignificant in the dissent model are set at their mean or modal values. When we compute the likelihood of our hypothetical judge issuing a dissent based on these assumed values, we find that the predicted probabilities are 0.43 for joining the majority opinion and 0.36 for writing a dissent (the remaining 0.21 probability is that associated with writing a concurrence). This simple calculation demonstrates that, while the baseline probability of observing a dissenting opinion is quite low and the effect of any single variable is minimal, a credible combination of factors results in a much higher likelihood of dissent. In terms of horizontal dissensus, this example makes clear that horizontal dissensus is more likely to be a fact of life when salient cases make their appearance on the docket and when active duty, nonfreshman judges are making the decisions in circuits lacking a norm of consensus.

To further illustrate our results, consider a case in which the ideological distance between a majority opinion writer and a potential separate opinion author is at its observed maximum and the separate opinion rate in that circuit is higher than average. We observe the maximum difference between the ideology scores for an individual judge and a majority opinion writer in the Court of Appeals for the Third Circuit in 1988 (the value on the ideological distance variable at this extreme is 1.16). In that circuit, the rate of separate opinions in 1987 was 17 percent, which is slightly above the average. To complete our calculations, we set the remaining variables at the same values as in the previous example. That is, our hypothesized judge is assumed to be a regular member of the circuit with at least two years of experience, who was appointed with an ABA rating below the well qualified level. We further assume that the case involves a civil rights issue, a third party filed an amicus brief, and the majority opinion reverses the lower court. Under these circumstances, the predicted probability of a dissent is about one in five. In other words, ideological distance, when combined with above average practices of separate opinion writing and other case characteristics, results in a probability of dissent more than four times the baseline.

In contrast, the conditions that minimize the probability of a dissent reduce the already-low baseline of observing a dissent to almost microscopic levels. The most extreme example of this occurs when an individual judge and the majority opinion writer have identical ideological preferences and work in a circuit with a very low propensity for issuing separate opinions. This combination occurs in the Court of Appeals for the Fourth Circuit in 1960. If we assume the judge in question is a district court judge serving by designation and who the ABA considered to be well qualified, and, further, that the case did not contain any of our indicators of salience or reverse the lower court decision, our model predicts the probability of dissent as functionally equivalent to zero (less than 0.01). Even if we remove the rather restrictive assumption that the judge is sitting by designation and instead assume the judge is the chief or is a freshman, we still obtain very low predicted probabilities of a dissent; a probability of merely 0.011 for the chief and only 0.014 for a freshman.

To demonstrate variations in the predicted probability of a concurrence, we make somewhat different assumptions than for the examples above, because different variables achieve statistical significance in our model of concurring opinions. The assumptions about ideological difference, separate opinion rate, civil rights or civil liberties issues, amicus briefs, and lower court reversal are the same, because these variables are significant in both models. For our example concerning the likelihood of concurrence, however, we assume that our hypothetical judge served on a state supreme court before her appointment to the court of appeals. Since there is no evidence that ABA rating affects the likelihood of a concurrence, however, we make no assumptions regarding the judge's ABA qualifications. We also allow the number of issues to vary but make no adjustments concerning our hypothetical judge's institutional role (as chief or freshman, for example).

Thus, for this first example the assumption is that the rate of separate opinions in the previous year is 41 percent and the ideological difference between our hypothetical judge and the majority opinion writer is 0.701. We further assume that the case involves a civil rights or civil liberties claim and that an amicus curiae brief was filed. Moreover, our hypothetical example assumes that the majority decision reverses the lower court and that the case is complex, with the number of issues involved set at the maximum observed in our data (seven). All other variables are set to their respective mean or modal values. Based on this combination of factors, the predicted probability of a concurrence increases to 0.59—a remarkable increase over the baseline of only 0.02.

The scenario that minimizes the probability of a concurrence assumes no ideological difference between the judge and the majority opinion writer in a circuit that issued separate opinions in fewer than 3 percent of its cases the prior year. The hypothetical case lacks any of the indicators of salience, complexity, or legal ambiguity such as civil rights or civil liberties claims, the presence of amicus briefs, numerous issues, or the reversal of the lower court. The individual judge is a regular serving, experienced member of the circuit who earned a well qualified rating from the ABA. Under these conditions, the predicted probability of a concurrence is less than 0.01. This result makes a great deal of intuitive sense. A concurrence usually reflects agreement with the outcome but disagreement with the reasoning. The case in this scenario lacks many of the factors that are likely to prompt a judge to craft a concurrence. The case is fairly simple; it lacks any of the obvious sources of alternative views, and the judge is not ideologically predisposed to view the world differently from the majority opinion writer. As a result, few judge, case, or institutional factors exist that would otherwise give rise to horizontal dissensus in the form of a concurrence.

Conclusion

The findings presented in this chapter indicate that judicial behavior on appellate courts is deeply embedded within, and structured by, judges' ideology, interpersonal relationships, and institutional context. Such behavior is also strongly affected by the nature of the case stimuli presented to the individual judge. Indeed, we noted that horizontal dissensus on the U.S. Courts of Appeals is a relatively rare phenomenon, especially when compared to the U.S. Supreme Court. Nevertheless, when the conditions are right, the probability of a dissent or concurrence in any given case can increase substantially.

Our findings also suggest that concurrences and dissents are not properly conceived as points along the same continuum of disagreement, but rather differ in important qualitative ways. For example, while both dissents and concurrences are functions of ideological disagreement, concurrences apparently do not threaten collegial relations to the same degree as dissents and are more often a function of case complexity than are dissents. Thus, there appear to be some important distinctions between the two forms of horizontal dissensus. In the next chapter, we turn to the question of whether appellate judges view dissents as a strategic tool for achieving their policy objectives.

Appendix

TABLE 3. Multinomial logit model of writing a concurrence or dissent

INDEPENDENT VARIABLE	COMPARISON: CONCUR–JOIN MAJORITY	ROBUST STANDARD ERROR	COMPARISON: DISSENT–JOIN MAJORITY	ROBUST STANDARD ERROR
Ideology				
Ideological disagreement (+)	0.551	0.163***	0.562	0.128***
Institutional roles				
Chief judge (–)	–0.040	0.196	–0.496	0.158***
Freshman judge (–)	–0.303	0.212	–0.272	0.139*
Designated district court judge (–)	–0.223	0.216	–0.916	0.195***
Senior judge (+)	–0.034	0.156	0.136	0.115
Judge characteristics				
Experience & prestige				
Prior federal court experience (+)	–0.156	0.133	0.010	0.087
Prior state supreme court experience (+)	0.414	0.186**	–0.214	0.156
ABA rating (–/+)	0.025	0.117	–0.231	0.084**
Case factors				
Salience				
Amicus curiae participation (+)	0.746	0.185***	0.426	0.159**
Civil rights/liberties claim (+)	0.260	0.151*	0.343	0.101***
Complexity				
Cross appeals (+)	0.060	0.223	0.176	0.144
Number of issues raised (+)	0.210	0.047***	0.030	0.038
Ambiguity				
Reversal (+)	0.257	0.124*	0.377	0.084***
Circuit characteristics				
Norms				
Separate opinion rate$_{t-1}$ (+)	6.33	0.808***	5.22	0.531***
Circuit size (+)	0.008	0.019	0.001	0.008
Opportunity				
Caseload (–)	–0.000	0.001	0.001	0.001
Constant	–5.340	0.252	–3.991	0.175

NOTE: N = 17,136; log likelihood = –4900.34; Wald $\chi^2_{(32)}$ = 393.70. Robust standard errors cluster on case citation. * $p < 0.05$, ** $p < 0.01$, *** $p < 0.001$ (one–tailed tests where directionality hypothesized).

TABLE 4. Descriptive statistics for variables in multinomial logit model of individual judge behavior

VARIABLE	MEAN	STANDARD DEVIATION	MINIMUM	MAXIMUM
Concurrence	0.031	0.173	0	1
Dissent	0.049	0.216	0	1
Ideological difference	0.364	0.296	0	1.16
Chief judge	0.085	0.280	0	1
Freshman judge	0.114	0.318	0	1
Designated judge	0.088	0.284	0	1
Senior judge	0.155	0.362	0	1
Prior federal court experience	0.378	0.485	0	1
Prior appellate court experience	0.083	0.276	0	1
ABA rating	0.631	0.483	0	1
Amicus curiae participation	0.042	0.202	0	1
Civil rights/liberties claim	0.145	0.353	0	1
Cross appeals	0.061	0.239	0	1
Number of issues raised	1.609	1.160	0	7
Reversal rate	0.300	0.458	0	1
Separate opinion rate (lagged)	0.132	0.066	0.019	0.409
Circuit size	11.04	4.950	3	28
Caseload	99.83	45.52	25.88	271.25

N = 17135

FOUR

The
Strategy
of
Dissent

In the previous chapter, we developed a model to explain a judge's decision to concur or dissent rather than join the majority opinion, and then subjected that model to empirical verification. In constructing that model, we drew first from the extensive literature scholars have produced demonstrating the importance of judges' attitudes in explaining their behavior. We proposed that the attitudes of judges would make a difference in the following way: the less the extent of shared values between a judge and a majority opinion author, the greater the likelihood of observing a separate opinion.

While recognizing the power of attitudes to explain such horizontal dissensus, we elaborated on the basic attitudinal explanation for separate opinion authorship by taking into account characteristics of the judges rendering decisions, the cases in which the judges are ruling, and the circuits within which they do so. When we compared our expectations to a sample of cases decided in the U.S. Courts of Appeals, we found that ideological differences between a judge and a majority opinion writer do matter. Additionally, the traits of judges, cases, and circuits also matter, although the pattern of effects differed for concurrences and dissents.

What we did not investigate in chapter 3, however, are two particular institutional features of the circuit courts that have the potential to further shape judicial behavior. The first of these features is the *en banc* proceeding in the courts of appeals. The second is the potential for appellate review by the U.S. Supreme Court. Both of these elements of institutional design mean that an individual on a three-judge panel who is unhappy

with the majority decision can take comfort in the fact that the panel decision may not be "the last word." Judges may engage in forward thinking
about the likely response to a panel decision by the circuit *en banc* or the
Supreme Court; such forward thinking may assist circuit judges in deciding the course of action most likely to satisfy their ideological preferences.
In other words, a judge might consider separate opinions, particularly dissenting opinions, as a strategic tool. Before we consider in greater detail
exactly when and how a circuit court judge can use dissent strategically,
we should first consider the meaning of "strategic action" and what scholars have uncovered thus far concerning strategic behavior by judges.

Both the attitudinal model and the strategic model of judicial behavior share a common assumption: judges seek to produce legal policy in
line with their own ideological preferences. While the strategic model begins with that assumption, however, it does not end there. According to
two leading scholars of the strategic model of judicial behavior, "justices
may be primarily seekers of legal policy, but they are not unconstrained
actors who make decisions based only on their own ideological attitudes.
Rather, justices are strategic actors who realize their ability to achieve their
goals depends on a consideration of the preferences of other actors, the
choices they expect others to make, and the institutional context in which
they act" (Epstein and Knight 1998, 10). In other words, to achieve the outcome most compatible with their policy preferences, judges consider the
impact of other judges' likely actions as well as their own. Depending on
the preferences of other relevant actors and how those actors are likely to
behave, a strategic judge might act differently than if his behavior was
driven by attitudinal considerations alone.

Scholars often point to Walter Murphy's *Elements of Judicial Strategy,*
published in 1964, as the classic or seminal work with regard to the strategic approach.[1] Murphy's interest was in answering the following question:
"How can a Justice of the Supreme Court most efficiently utilize his resources, official and personal, to achieve a particular set of policy objectives?" (1964, 3–4). Relying on a rich trove of information mined from the
papers of numerous justices, Murphy developed an answer to this question that, in part, relied a great deal on the justices' considerations of their
colleagues' preferences. Although little research engaging this strategic
line of inquiry immediately followed Murphy's book,[2] the strategic model
emerged as a prominent analytical framework in the 1990s. In fact, as one
student of the courts has observed, "One of the pivotal debates in the literature on U.S. courts is the extent to which judges can and do act strategically vis-à-vis other actors" (Langer 2002, 14).

In taking into account the preferences of others, a strategic judge might find that his objectives differ from those of other actors involved in the decision-making process. Such a judge recognizes that future action by those actors may foil the realization of his own preferred outcome. A judge in this situation might suppress his ideological inclinations out of concern that following those inclinations in the short term would lead to a less desirable outcome in the long term. Alternatively, a judge may recognize that a larger policy goal and/or a longer-term policy solution may be accomplished because she shares policy preferences with other relevant actors. In that fortuitous circumstance, this judge would have an increased incentive to express her ideological preferences in the short run.

Careful work by a variety of scholars has provided evidence that judges, operating in a range of different courts, act strategically in this manner. For example, Saul Brenner and John Krol (1989); Gregory Caldeira, John Wright, and Christopher Zorn (1999); and Charles Cameron, Jeffrey Segal, and Donald Songer (2000) have all examined Supreme Court justices' decision making in the agenda-setting (certiorari) process and found evidence of strategic behavior. Work by Laura Langer (1997, 1999) also focused, in part, on agenda setting, though her concern was with the behavior of state courts of last resort. She, too, documented strategic behavior by judges. In the U.S. Supreme Court and state supreme courts, judges appear to structure their choices regarding docket composition based on what they anticipate other relevant actors will do. Strategic accounts have also been offered—and empirically verified—regarding majority opinion assignment and writing (Epstein and Knight 1998, 95–106; Maltzman, Spriggs, and Wahlbeck 2000). Of special interest for our purposes is the extant work on strategy and dissenting behavior.

Dissent as a Strategic Tool

Arguably, the most extensive work concerning the strategic use of dissent focuses on state courts of last resort. Paul Brace and Melinda Gann Hall, in particular, undertook a series of studies examining dissenting behavior by state supreme court justices at both the aggregate level (Brace and Hall 1990; Hall and Brace 1989) and the individual judge level (Brace and Hall 1993; Hall and Brace 1992). Key to their efforts in this regard is their consideration of state supreme court justices' particular institutional and political contexts. Brace and Hall highlight the potential for (and actual effect of) different judicial selection mechanisms to structure the expression of dissent. For example, judges who might otherwise vote to strike down death sentences may find their inclination to do so reduced in the presence of negative electoral consequences.[3]

Work by Paul Wahlbeck, James Spriggs, and Forrest Maltzman (1999) also reveals strategic motivations underlying separate opinion-writing behavior on the U.S. Supreme Court. In their study of the Burger Court, Wahlbeck and his colleagues developed a portrait of the justices' calculations regarding separate opinion authorship that takes into account strategic factors, such as past cooperation on the part of majority opinion writers. On this point, they found that justices often consider the past behavior of the majority opinion writer when deciding whether to file a separate opinion. They ultimately concluded, "Our analysis lends credence to the view that Supreme Court justices are rational actors who pursue their policy goals within constraints—strategic and institutional factors temper justices' pursuit of policy preferences" (1999, 507). In other words, Supreme Court justices' decisions whether to concur or dissent are often shaped by strategic considerations.

Considered collectively, this work on the strategic motivations underlying justices' decisions to file separate opinions on state supreme courts and the U.S. Supreme Court is quite suggestive with respect to the potential for such strategic behavior on the U.S Courts of Appeals. After all, if jurists on state appellate tribunals and the nation's highest appellate court engage in such behavior, why not circuit court judges? Although circuit court judges operate with different institutional rules than justices on appellate courts of last resort, certain institutional mechanisms at the circuit court provide judges with the opportunity to act strategically. A three-judge panel ruling is not necessarily the final word because that panel decision may be reviewed and reversed by the circuit as a whole or the U.S. Supreme Court. Accordingly, the potential exists for a dissenting judge to signal both the circuit *en banc* and the Supreme Court to persuade those reviewing bodies to reverse the panel decision. This means that a judge unhappy with the ruling of a panel on which she is a member can (potentially) get, not just a second bite at the apple, but a third bite, too!

Of course, a judge's ability to signal the circuit or the Supreme Court presupposes that a dissent from a panel decision carries significant meaning for those judicial actors external to the panel. With regard to the circuit, both Tracey George (1999) and Douglas Ginsburg and Donald Falk (1991) provide evidence that dissents do matter in terms of structuring *en banc* review. In both studies, the authors found that the presence of dissent enhanced the likelihood that the circuit would grant *en banc* review. Further, persuasive evidence exists regarding the Supreme Court's case-

selection process to suggest that lower court dissent has significant meaning for the justices as well. Supreme Court justices must wade through
thousands of certiorari petitions each year to identify likely candidates for
review. The literature devoted to that process is quite substantial.[4] One insight gleaned from that body of work is that dissensus in the lower court—
that is, horizontal dissensus, as evidenced by a dissenting opinion—significantly increases the likelihood that the Court will place a case on its
limited docket (Caldeira, Wright, and Zorn 1999).

Social science has thus demonstrated that a panel member's dissent affects decision making at both the circuit *en banc* and the Supreme Court.
The question remains whether circuit judges consciously use dissents
strategically so as to trigger certain responses by these reviewing bodies.
Two studies exist that are directly on point. First, Steven Van Winkle
(1997) tested a signaling model of the decision to dissent. He argued that
members of a three-judge panel who find themselves at odds with their fellow panelists and who share similar proclivities with the circuit majority
will be more likely to file a dissent, in hope of signaling the circuit that the
panel is behaving contrary to the circuit's preferences and thereby trigger-
ing *en banc* review. Van Winkle evaluated his signaling theory using data
on search and seizure decisions issued by the U.S. Courts of Appeals during the 1992–93 period and found evidence in support of his strategic account. Second, in our earlier work (Hettinger, Lindquist, and Martinek
2004), we searched for empirical evidence that judges articulate or suppress
dissents based on their predictions concerning the outcome of full circuit
review. Unlike Van Winkle, we found no empirical support for strategic
behavior of this sort. The explanation for these discrepant results may be
that Van Winkle examined only a single issue area (search and seizure) over
a limited time period, while we focused on strategic behavior across the full
range of cases on circuit court dockets over a much longer time period.[5]

With regard to dissent as a strategic tool to signal the Supreme Court,
at least one study offers empirical insight into this question. Frank Cross
and Emerson Tiller (1998) evaluated how the composition of an appeals
court panel might affect the behavior of individual panel members. The
authors' substantive focus involved rulings implicating judicial deference
to decisions by administrative agencies in light of Supreme Court precedent mandating such deference. They found that when a panel contained
a potential whistleblower who agreed with the High Court's precedent—
and who might "blow the whistle" by dissenting from the majority opinion—the panel decision was more likely to adhere to that precedent. This
finding suggests that judges on the U.S. Courts of Appeals might well

view the threat of dissent as a strategic tool suitable for signaling the Supreme Court regarding noncompliant panel decisions.

Institutional features of the U.S. Courts of Appeals may therefore provide a strategic circuit judge with certain opportunities to pursue her policy objectives beyond persuading her fellow panelists to adopt her point of view. First, the possibility of *en banc* review of three-judge panel decisions may encourage a judge to file a dissenting opinion to highlight the panel ruling's incongruence with circuit preferences. Second, review by the Supreme Court provides the strategic judge with the opportunity to file a dissenting opinion as a means to enhance the likelihood of Supreme Court review. Moreover, the available empirical evidence suggests, first, that dissent plays a role in both the circuit decision to grant *en banc* review and the Supreme Court decision to grant the writ of certiorari and, second, that courts of appeals jurists at least sometimes do act strategically in this regard (although the evidence is mixed on this last point). In the next section, we develop a strategic model of a judge's decision to file a dissent, which we subsequently use to evaluate whether the empirical evidence supports a strategic account of dissents.

Constructing a Strategic Model of Dissents on the U.S. Courts of Appeals

As we demonstrated in the previous chapter, and as others have demonstrated previously, divergence between a judge's ideological preferences and those of the majority opinion writer increases the likelihood of dissent. Simply put, ideological disagreement motivates judges to expend the resources necessary to write a dissenting opinion. We now focus on the question of whether a strategic account provides additional insights into the decision to file a dissent beyond this basic attitudinal explanation. Ultimately, we are interested in a judge's strategic behavior vis-à-vis both the circuit *en banc* and the Supreme Court. In either case, essential to the decision calculus of a potential (strategic) dissenter are his preferences, those of the majority opinion writer, and those of the actors with the power to review the panel decision (the circuit *en banc* and the Supreme Court, respectively). The relative distances between and among three sets of preferences—those of the majority opinion writer, the potential dissenter, and the potential reviewing body—form the foundation for a judge's strategic calculations concerning whether to dissent.

A judge deciding whether to dissent has some information about the preferences of each relevant actor. First, he knows his own preferences. Second, since he was a participant in the panel decision, he knows what ideological position the majority decision represents. As in the previous chapter, we assume that the preferences of the majority opinion writer represent the ideological position taken in the majority opinion. A judge contemplating a dissenting opinion also has a good idea about the likely outcome of review by the circuit *en banc* or the Supreme Court. This idea is based on his prior experiences as a member of the circuit and his observations regarding the Supreme Court. Depending on the configuration of those preferences (i.e., those of the judge [J], the majority opinion writer [MOW], and the reviewing body [R]), a strategic judge will be more or less likely to dissent in order to invite subsequent review and reversal.

To illustrate how the configuration of preferences matters, we can think about them as falling along a liberal-conservative ideological continuum. A judge may find himself in three situations. Regardless of which scenario described below obtains, a judge's basic motivation to dissent is represented by the distance between his ideological preferences and those of the majority opinion writer. In the first situation, the majority opinion author's (MOW) position falls somewhere between that of the judge (J) and the reviewing body (R), either (R < MOW < J) or (J < MOW < R):

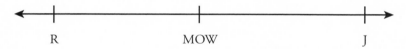

Under these conditions, a judge is better off with the panel decision than he would be if the circuit or Supreme Court intervened and reviewed the panel decision, because, if review occurred, the outcome would fall at R, which is farther away from J than MOW. MOW may be quite far away from J's preferred position, but an outcome at R resulting from review by the circuit *en banc* or the Supreme Court is even more distant. Moreover, since a decision by the circuit *en banc* or the Supreme Court has greater precedential significance, the judge would not only end up worse off in this case, but also in many future cases as well. Thus, while the judge's ideological disagreement with the panel decision prompts a desire to dissent, that desire might be diminished by her calculation that the outcome of review might be even more undesirable from her perspective in the long run.

Second, a potential dissenter can find herself in a situation in which the preferences of R fall somewhere between those of J and MOW, either (J < R < MOW) or (MOW < R < J):

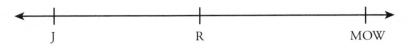

Once again, based on the distance between the panel decision and her preferred outcome, the judge has an ideological incentive to dissent. Unlike in the previous scenario, however, here the judge has an added incentive to dissent based on her position relative to the panel decision and the likely outcome of review. A judge thinking ahead to a future outcome by the reviewing body can see that, if review were to occur, that outcome would be closer to her preferred position than that represented by MOW.

The most complicated calculation for a judge occurs when her preferences fall between those of the majority opinion writer and the potential reviewing body, either (R < J < MOW) or (MOW < J < R):

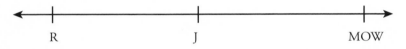

Key to the judge's calculations about whether she should dissent to signal either the circuit *en banc* or the Supreme Court is how close she is to the reviewing body relative to the MOW. When the potential dissenter is closer to R than to MOW, a forward-thinking judge will have an added incentive to dissent, because the outcome of such review will be closer to J than the existing panel decision. Conversely, when the potential dissenter is closer to MOW than R, a forward-thinking judge will be faced with a disincentive to dissent, because review, if it occurs, will put the final outcome even farther away from J's preferred position than the position represented by the panel decision.

Up to this point, we have considered how the relative positions of a judge, majority opinion author, and reviewing body might come into play in the calculations of a judge vis-à-vis filing or suppressing a dissent. But not all disagreements a judge might have with a panel decision are likely to be significant enough to give rise to strategic calculations. To see this, we can think about the ideological difference between a judge and a majority opinion author as representing the policy "loss" for the judge. When that policy loss is small or negligible, a rational judge is less likely to feel compelled to expend the time to strategically calculate the costs or benefits of a dissent. Conversely, the greater that policy loss is, the greater the impetus a judge has to make that calculation. In other words, *the extent of ideological disagreement between a judge and a majority opinion writer conditions a judge's strategic calculations.*

Estimating a Strategic Model of Dissents
on the U.S. Courts of Appeals

As discussed above, theoretically, a judge's decision to file a dissenting opinion may be a function of ideological disagreement with the panel decision coupled with strategic calculations regarding the outcome of review by the circuit *en banc* or the Supreme Court—conditioned by the extent of the initial ideological disagreement. Our purpose in this section is to subject this theoretical account to empirical testing. To do so, we construct a model that incorporates both the attitudinal and strategic components we outlined above. Before proceeding, however, an important note is in order. While our concern in chapter 3 was with the decision to file a separate opinion, whether that separate opinion was a concurrence or dissent, in this chapter we limit our focus to the decision to file a dissenting opinion.

Our overarching interest in this book is with the expression of dissensus—both horizontal and vertical—and both concurrences and dissents represent a form of horizontal dissensus. Nevertheless, concurrences are much less likely candidates than dissents for purposes of strategic signaling. Since the authors of concurring opinions at the U.S. Courts of Appeals largely (or even entirely) agree with the majority opinion author regarding the case outcome, they have less incentive to encourage review by either the circuit or the Supreme Court. Accordingly, to evaluate whether strategic calculations are at play with regard to horizontal dissensus, a focus on dissents is most appropriate.

To evaluate the strategic account articulated above, we need a measure of ideology that is comparable among and between circuit court judges and Supreme Court justices along the ideological dimension we have hypothesized. We start with the measure of circuit court judge preferences. As outlined in chapter 3, Micheal Giles, Virginia Hettinger, and Todd Peppers (2002) demonstrated the important role of senatorial courtesy in the selection of jurists for the circuit bench. Based on that evidence, and in conjunction with Keith Poole's (1998) work measuring the ideology of legislators and presidents, the resulting measure of circuit judge ideology suggested by Giles and his colleagues is as follows: when neither home-state senator is of the president's party, the judge's ideology score is equal to that of the president; when there is one home-state senator of the president's party, the judge's ideology score is equal to that of that senator; and, when there are two home-state senators of the president's party, the judge's ideology score is equal to the average of the two senators' scores. As in chapter 3, we use the absolute value of the difference of the judge's score and the majority opinion writer's score to represent the basic attitudinal disagreement between the two. The greater this difference, the more likely is a dissent.

We can use this same measure to devise an indicator of the outcome in the event of *en banc* review by the circuit. A reasonable approximation of that outcome is the position of the median member of the circuit. This median value for the full circuit's preferences provides all the elements we need to construct a variable indicating when a potential dissenter has an *enhanced* incentive to dissent even beyond the basic attitudinal disagreement between him and the majority opinion writer. It also provides us with the information necessary to construct a variable indicating when a potential dissenter has a *diminished* incentive to dissent, despite the basic attitudinal disagreement between him and the majority opinion writer. For simplicity's sake, we will refer to the former as the "circuit enhancement variable" and the latter as the "circuit diminishment variable."

The circuit enhancement variable is equal to the absolute value of the difference between the majority opinion writer and the circuit median whenever a judge has reason to believe that a circuit intervention will result in a final outcome more amenable to his preferred outcome than that represented by the panel decision—that is, when the judge is closer to the circuit median than the majority opinion writer. Under those conditions, if the ideological distance between a judge and the panel decision represents a policy "loss" by the potential dissenter, the ideological distance between the majority opinion writer and the circuit median represents the policy "gain" experienced by the judge in the event of circuit intervention in the form of *en banc* review. We can use the same logic to develop the circuit diminishment variable. Under those conditions in which *en banc* review will result in a final outcome that is even worse for a judge than the panel decision—that is, when the judge is closer to the majority opinion writer than the circuit median—the ideological difference between the majority opinion writer and the circuit median represents an even greater policy "loss" to the judge than that represented by the panel decision. Hence, a judge in that situation has a diminished incentive to dissent.

To evaluate the notion that judges will expend the necessary time and energy to engage in strategic calculations only when it is worth it (i.e., when the judge's preferred outcome is very distant from that of the majority opinion writer), we can include "interaction terms." Interaction terms simply reflect the extent to which the impact of one variable is conditioned by the values of another variable. In this case, we first interact our variable measuring the ideological distance between the judge and majority opinion writer with the circuit enhancement variable, and, second, interact the same ideological distance variable with the circuit diminishment variable. The first interaction is designed to provide some insight into whether judges are more likely to engage in strategic calculations the more they have at stake in terms of their likely policy gain. The second interaction is designed to do the same for the question of whether judges are more likely to do so when they have more to lose.

We also need to devise a similar methodological approach with regard to judge, panel, and Supreme Court preferences. We do so by using the approach devised by Giles, Hettinger, and Peppers (2002) to measure Supreme Court justice preferences as well. Senatorial courtesy is not a factor in the Supreme Court appointment process; hence a reasonable approximation of a justice's ideology is that of the president who appointed him. And, a reasonable approximation of the outcome in the event of Supreme Court review is the preference of the median member of that body. Accordingly, we assigned each justice the ideology score corresponding to that developed by Poole for his or her appointing president. We then use the median member's score to represent the likely outcome of Supreme Court review. From here, we construct measures of Supreme Court enhancement and Supreme Court diminishment that parallel the circuit court enhancement and circuit court diminishment measures described above. Further, we include comparable interaction terms to assess the conditioning effect on strategic behavior of *the extent of* the judge's ideological disagreement with the panel decision.

To evaluate this strategic account of dissenting behavior, we use a subset of the data we employed in chapter 3. In this chapter, we use the data available in the Songer Database from 1971 up to and including 1996. This more limited, but still lengthy, period of time was necessary for practical reasons: the data necessary to measure the ideology of Supreme Court justices, and thereby ascertain the Court median, is limited and therefore precluded our use of earlier years.

We are interested in a judge's decision to select from a set of two choices: either to file a dissent or not. When an outcome can take on only one of two values, the MNL estimation technique we employed in chapter 3 simplifies to the less-complex logit model, which we use here. Just as with the MNL model, it is very easy to get an intuitive sense about which variables matter and whether they make the decision to file a dissent more

TABLE 5. Summary of strategic dissent model

VARIABLE	EFFECT
Ideology	
Ideological disagreement	Dissent *more* likely
Strategy regarding the circuit	
Circuit enhancement	No effect
Circuit diminishment	No effect
Circuit enhancement conditional on ideological disagreement	No effect
Circuit diminishment conditional on ideological disagreement	No effect
Strategy regarding the Supreme Court	
Supreme Court enhancement	No effect
Supreme Court diminishment	No effect
Supreme Court enhancement conditional on ideological disagreement	No effect
Supreme Court diminishment conditional on ideological disagreement	No effect

or less likely. Table 5 summarizes the results from estimating the logit model, but the full statistical results (including alternative specifications and descriptive statistics) are reported in the appendix to this chapter.

As table 5 reports, although the basic attitudinal disagreement between a judge and majority opinion author matters, we find no evidence that strategic considerations come into play in the decision to file a dissenting opinion, whether vis-à-vis the circuit *en banc* or the Supreme Court.[6] The fact that attitudinal disagreement alone matters should come as no surprise, especially in light of the analysis presented in chapter 3. The fact that strategic considerations matter not at all, however, presents a stark contrast to evidence regarding strategic dissenting behavior at the U.S. Supreme Court and in state courts of last resort. Moreover, these results are not merely an artifact of our modeling strategy incorporating considerations concerning both reviewing bodies. Whether we evaluate circuit judges' strategic calculations solely with regard to the circuit *en banc* or solely with regard to the Supreme Court, we still find no evidence to support a strategic account of the decision to dissent. (See table 6, models 1 and 2.)

A series of alternative estimations likewise failed to yield such evidence. For example, some might argue that a judge behaves strategically with regard to the decision to file a dissent only if strategic calculations lead her to be less likely to dissent than she otherwise would; that is, the

TABLE 6. Alternative logit model of the decision to dissent

VARIABLE	MODEL 1	MODEL 2	MODEL 3
Constant	−3.176**	−3.253**	−3.265**
	(0.097)	(0.126)	(0.110)
Ideology			
Ideological disagreement	0.863**	0.648*	0.748**
	(0.208)	(0.233)	(0.176)
Strategy regarding the circuit			
Circuit enhancement	−0.314	—	—
	(0.562)		
Circuit diminishment	0.234	—	0.287
	(0.387)		(0.401)
Circuit enhancement conditional			
on ideological disagreement	−0.044	—	—
	(0.679)		
Circuit diminishment conditional			
on ideological disagreement	−0.860	—	−1.683
	(2.220)	—	(2.293)
Strategy regarding the Supreme Court			
Supreme Court enhancement	—	0.185	—
		(0.705)	
Supreme Court diminishment	—	0.174	0.120
		(0.299)	(0.294)
Supreme Court enhancement condi-			
tional on ideological disagreement	—	−0.022	—
		(0.779)	
Supreme Court diminishment condi-			
tional on ideological disagreement	—	1.555	1.580
		(1.034)	(1.015)
Log likelihood	−2522.19	−2519.87	−2519.88
Wald χ^2	24.69	27.10	27.19

NOTE: N = 12291, robust standard errors cluster on citation. * $p < 0.005$, ** $p < 0.000$

circuit enhancement and Supreme Court enhancement variables only serve to reinforce existing proclivities to dissent and, accordingly, do not represent strategic behavior on the part of judges. But, even when we estimate a model including only those variables hypothesized to reduce a judge's likelihood of dissenting, we still find no evidence supporting the strategic account. (See table 6, model 3.)

Conclusion

In this chapter, we presented a theoretical model of strategic dissenting behavior by circuit court judges and subjected that model to empirical evaluation using a straightforward statistical model accounting for various configurations of preferences among a potential dissenting judge, majority opinion writer, and reviewing body. Yet we found no evidence of strategic behavior in cases across the board. This finding does not rule out the possibility that some judges do, indeed, act strategically with respect to other aspects of the decision-making process. But it does suggest that, in general, circuit court judges do not act strategically when choosing to dissent.

Why do circuit judges differ from state and federal supreme court justices in this regard? One obvious difference between circuit and supreme court justices is that many state supreme courts and the U.S. Supreme Court enjoy largely discretionary rather than mandatory dockets. Thus, circuit court judges may simply have less time to engage in the strategic calculations described in our theoretical model. In addition, research by David Klein and Robert Hume (2003) indicates that circuit court judges take little account of potential Supreme Court action on appeals from circuit rulings, as circuit judges exhibit no "fear of reversal" that has behavioral manifestations. The same pattern may obtain here, in that circuit judges simply dissent when it suits them ideologically and then let the chips fall where they may.

Appendix

TABLE 7. Full logit model of the decision to dissent

VARIABLE	COEFFICIENT	ROBUST STANDARD ERROR
Constant	−3.267	0.132*
Ideology		
Ideological disagreement	0.782	0.261*
Strategy regarding the circuit		
Circuit enhancement	−0.092	0.652
Circuit diminishment	0.307	0.404
Circuit enhancement conditional on ideological disagreement	−0.222	0.853
Circuit diminishment conditional on ideological disagreement	−2.143	2.330
Strategy regarding the Supreme Court		
Supreme Court enhancement	0.120	0.797
Supreme Court diminishment	0.113	0.311
Supreme Court enhancement conditional on ideological disagreement	0.115	0.934
Supreme Court diminishment conditional on ideological disagreement	1.706	1.119

NOTE: N = 12291; log likelihood = −2519.05; Wald χ^2 = 29.32. Robust standard errors clustered on case citation. * $p < 0.001$.

TABLE 8. Descriptive statistics for variables included in the strategic model of the decision to dissent

VARIABLE	MEAN	STANDARD DEVIATION	MINIMUM	MAXIMUM
Dissent	0.056	0.229	0	1.000
Ideological disagreement	0.371	0.302	0	1.158
Circuit enhancement	0.172	0.228	0	1.078
Circuit diminishment	0.067	0.154	0	1.103
Circuit enhancement conditional on ideological disagreement	0.112	0.194	0	1.162
Circuit diminishment conditional on ideological disagreement	0.007	0.022	0	0.229
Supreme Court enhancement	0.133	0.243	0	1.136
Supreme Court diminishment	0.195	0.253	0	1.056
Supreme Court enhancement conditional on ideological disagreement	0.095	0.212	0	1.290
Supreme Court diminishment conditional on ideological disagreement	0.033	0.054	0	0.329

FIVE

The
Decision
to Reverse

As discussed in chapter 2, the hierarchical nature of the federal judiciary creates different forms of decision-making authority at its first two levels. While both district and circuit court judges are undoubtedly concerned with the smooth (and "correct") operation of the judicial system, their responsibilities in this regard differ. The federal district courts constitute the primary trial courts in the federal system. District court judges therefore serve as the first and, in most instances, the only point of contact for litigants. Jurists on the U.S. Courts of Appeals, however, handle no pretrial negotiations and conduct no trials. Instead, they review lower court or administrative agency decisions for error. Created specifically to relieve pressures on the U.S. Supreme Court, the U.S. Courts of Appeals have become the de facto (if not the de jure) venue for final appellate review. For virtually all litigants who seek review, these courts are the first and last stop in the appellate process.

Working in tandem, the district courts and the circuit courts handle all but a comparatively trivial number of federal court cases. Their different roles in that process have the potential to engender dissensus between district and circuit judges, which we have labeled vertical dissensus. That is not to say that conflict is inevitable in any given case. Despite the different functions for which each is responsible, the district courts and courts of appeals may often find that fulfilling their respective functions does not result in much disagreement. Even a casual perusal of the data pertaining to circuit court reversal of district court decisions makes clear that conflict between the district and circuit court level does not arise in the majority of cases. As Donald Songer, Reginald Sheehan, and Susan Haire (2000) report, based on data from cases with published opinions, the rate of district court reversal across all circuits has hovered between approximately 25 percent and 30 percent.[1] When all terminations on the merits are considered, whether or not resulting in a published opinion, the data indicate an even lower reversal rate. In the statistical year ending in September 2003, for example, the circuits reversed 9.1 percent of all cases heard on the merits, with reversal rates per circuit ranging from a low of 1.1 percent in the Second Circuit to a high of 14.9 percent in the D.C. Circuit in that year.[2]

Although reversal occurs only in a minority of cases, its importance to the circuit court as a tool for error correction and policy formation cannot be gainsaid. Error correction via appellate court review is a critical function of any appellate system. It is, perhaps, the most important such function and is paramount for ensuring consistency in the law (especially in the presence of a rogue trial judge). Conversely, because they disturb at least one previously settled legal matter, reversals can also result in perceived or actual legal inconsistency. Reversal can thus pose a threat to the consistency of the law if it is used as a mechanism for the pursuit of individual judges' ideological goals without concern for legal predictability.

As noted above, circuit judges use their power of reversal somewhat sparingly. Circuit judges' reluctance to reverse is likely related, at least in part, to their preference for more, rather than less, harmonious relations with lower court judges. After all, circuit and district court judges serve together on the circuit's Judicial Council and on committees of the Judicial Conference,[3] as well as on appellate panels from time to time. In addition, many circuit court judges are elevated from the district court and thereafter find themselves reviewing the work of their former district court colleagues. As a result, appeals court judges are likely to prefer to affirm rather than reverse the district court ruling.

Given its critical function in the administration of justice and its implications for collegiality and efficiency, reversal is an important phenomenon to understand. In the next section, we set forth our theoretical expectations regarding circuit panels' propensity to reverse, discuss the measurement of our theoretical concepts, and then evaluate those theoretical expectations empirically using data from the U.S. Courts of Appeals, 1960 to 1996.

Theoretical Expectations Regarding the Panel Decision to Reverse

The decision of a circuit panel to upset a lower court ruling is likely a function of systematic forces related to ideology, institutional roles, case factors, and circuit characteristics. We begin with the most prominent of these potential explanations, the attitudinal model.

ATTITUDES AND LOWER COURT REVERSAL. As the legal realists and attitudinal theorists have made eminently clear, judicial decision making is not immune from the influence of judges' personal preferences. The empirical evidence presented in chapters 3 and 4, as well as the extant literature (e.g., Howard 1981; Rowland and Carp 1996), demonstrates that district and circuit court judges are motivated by their own policy preferences. These policy preferences shape judges' interpretations of the law, including how the law determines appropriate case outcomes. When considering a circuit panel's decision whether to reverse a district court judgment, then, it stands to reason that when the policy preferences of the reviewing panel are at odds with those of the district court judge who presided in the case below, the likelihood of disagreement over proper case resolution increases. In other words, where policy or ideological preferences between circuit and district court diverge, opinions regarding the application and interpretation of legal principles will similarly diverge, resulting in conflict over case outcomes. In such situations, the circuit panel may choose to reverse.

For purposes of evaluating the decision to reverse empirically, we use the circuit panel, rather than the individual circuit judge, as the unit of analysis. As in previous chapters, to measure panel ideology we relied on the Micheal Giles, Virginia Hettinger, and Todd Peppers (2002) ideological scores for the majority opinion writer.[4] We also applied the Giles, Hettinger, and Peppers methodology to derive a measure of ideology for district court judges and used the resulting measures to compute the arithmetic difference between the scores for the circuit panel and district court judge below. We expect that the larger that difference, the greater the distance between the ideological propensities of the district and circuit courts, and the more likely reversal will be.

INSTITUTIONAL ROLES. We noted above that, all else being equal, circuit judges are likely to prefer harmonious relations with district court judges. But there are good reasons to suspect that some courts of appeals judges have enhanced sensibilities in this regard, which may be manifested in a reduced likelihood to reverse the lower court. If these judges are members of a reviewing three-judge circuit court panel, their disinclination to reverse may depress the likelihood of reversal by that panel. We hypothesize that two institutional roles, in particular, are likely to affect a panel's decision to reverse: the chief judge and district court judges sitting by designation.[5]

Recall that chief judges are those actors with the primary administrative responsibilities for their respective circuits and, as such, they are charged with a diverse set of duties. Attention to these responsibilities is likely to reinforce for chief judges the importance of the smooth functioning of the circuit and thus make them especially sensitive to anything that can compromise the efficient operation of the circuit, including reversals of the lower court. The chief judge's administrative responsibilities also give him unique insights into the work of a district court judge. This heightened familiarity with and sensitivity to the workload and responsibilities of a district court judge may make the chief judge loathe to reverse a district court ruling unless absolutely necessary.

The chief judge may feel a countervailing pressure with regard to reversal, however. The chief judge's administrative responsibilities for case processing in the circuit may also enhance his sensitivity to error correction. While reversal in a particular case may generate additional work related to that case, systemic failure to correct error may, in general, compromise legal stability and efficient case processing in the future. Litigants may attempt to capitalize on a persistent pattern of error at the district court level and bring what would otherwise be considered nonmeritorious claims. Moreover, in the presence of uncertainty caused by inconsistent error correction by the circuit court, litigants dissatisfied at the trial level may pursue an appeal when they might not otherwise do so. In short, chief judges' responsibilities for efficient case processing at both the district and circuit court levels may generate conflicting pressures when it comes to reversals. Thus, while we suspect that the role of chief judge may affect the propensity to reverse, we have no a priori expectations regarding the direction of the impact.

Of course, when a chief judge is serving on a particular panel, he is only one of the three members of that panel and, hence, does not have the authority alone to dictate whether the panel reverses the district court. Arguably, however, the chief judge can be most influential in this regard when he is the majority opinion author. Even when he is not the majority opinion author, however, the chief judge's mere presence on the panel gives him the opportunity to persuade his colleagues. In other words, a chief judge may influence the likelihood of a panel reversing the lower court whether he authors the majority opinion or is simply a member of the panel, though his influence is likely to be stronger in the former case.

This discussion of the chief judge's likely influence regarding lower court reversal would be moot, however, if, in practice, the chief judge had few opportunities to act on those preferences. It is true that there is only a single chief judge on a circuit at any given time and there are myriad three-judge panel combinations possible in even the smallest circuit. Even so, our data from 1960 to 1996 reveal that chief judges serve as majority opinion authors in a nontrivial percentage of cases—approximately 8 percent of the time—and are members of three-judge panels without authoring the majority opinion in slightly more than 16 percent of cases. Thus, ample opportunities exist for chief judges to influence the decision to reverse the district court, whether as a panel member or the majority opinion author.

The role of chief judge is not the only institutional identity likely to influence the decision to reverse. An increasing number of courts of appeals decisions are rendered with the assistance of designated district court judges. As discussed in chapter 2, the chief judge of a panel may assign a district court judge from within the circuit to serve temporarily as an appellate judge. District court judges perform fundamentally different functions than appeals court judges, a fact reflected in the very process by which the federal bench is staffed. Presidents and senators see judgeships for the district and appeals courts differently, as manifested in the differential selection and treatment of nominees to these two benches (Goldman 1997; Martinek, Kemper, and Van Winkle 2002). Despite the fact that district court judges are not assigned to review cases arising from their own district (Brudney and Ditslear 2001, 573), they nonetheless remain district court judges reviewing the work of their peers. Hence, it is not unreasonable to suppose that "[w]hen district court judges are appointed to appellate panels they approach their task with divided loyalty" (Green and Atkins 1978, 368). The question remains, however, whether district court judges actually behave differently when sitting on the circuit courts with respect to reversal. Some persuasive empirical evidence exists that suggests they do, at least in certain case categories (Brudney and Ditslear 2001, evaluating labor cases; Haire, Lindquist, and Songer 2003, evaluating civil liberties cases).

As with chief judges, the influence of a designated district court judge on the likelihood of reversal may arise either from her authorship of the majority opinion or her simple presence on the three-judge circuit panel. In the former case, the district court judge may use her substantial influence over the content of the majority opinion to move the panel away from reversal. In the latter, she may simply employ her powers of persuasion to convince her colleagues as to the wisdom of affirmance. Alternatively, even if the designated judge makes no efforts in that direction, her mere presence may enhance other panel members' deference to the lower court.

As is the case with chief judges, district court judges sitting by designation often have the opportunity to exercise influence. District court judges wrote the majority opinion in 7 percent of the cases we analyze later in this chapter and served in a non-opinion writing role on another 19 percent of all panels. Moreover, unlike our expectations regarding the influence of chief judges on reversal, we have good reason to anticipate clear directional relationships between reversals and the presence of district court judges on the panel (as opinion writers or otherwise). We expect that a panel will be less likely to reverse a lower court decision if a district court judge sitting by designation authors the majority opinion and, further, that a panel will be less likely to reverse a lower court decision if a district court judge sitting by designation is a member.

CASE FACTORS. Ideological disagreement and institutional roles are judge-centered characteristics with important consequences for lower court reversal. But these are not the only characteristics likely to structure the expression of disagreement between a district court judge and a reviewing circuit panel. Characteristics of the case are also important. For the panel decision to reverse, three case characteristics are of special interest: salience, complexity, and the quality of the legal argument.

Salient cases are those that a circuit court judge is likely to evaluate as meriting closer attention. As discussed in detail in chapter 3, two indicators of case salience are the presence of amicus curiae briefs and civil rights or civil liberties claims.[6] Amicus briefs indicate external interest in the case outcome, while the existence of a civil rights or civil liberties claim reflects the important substantive values implicated by the decision. Both are likely to prompt judges on the U.S. Courts of Appeals to devote careful attention to the record that may reveal error below, thereby leading to reversal.

If salience has to do with the decision to reverse from the perspective of the reviewing panel, complexity has more to do with the ability of district court judges to avoid reversible error. Stated simply, the more complex a case, the more easily a district court judge can arrive at an erroneous ruling.[7] As discussed in chapter 3, two appropriate measures of complexity are the presence of cross appeals and the number of legal issues raised.[8] Cross appeals provide appellate judges with more grounds to reverse, as both parties to the dispute below are unhappy with some element of the outcome. Similarly, we speculate that, as the number of issues raised on appeal increases, the greater the likelihood of reversal, as more complex, multifaceted cases give appellate judges more grounds on which to disagree with the lower court ruling.

A final case characteristic to consider has to do with the quality of the legal argument. As the intermediate courts in the federal judicial hierarchy, the circuit courts serve as the forum in which litigants can generally appeal as of right. This mandatory docket gives rise to more frivolous or noncontroversial appeals than would a discretionary docket. As a consequence, circuit courts are more likely to affirm the lower court ruling in most cases. To overcome this presumption in favor of affirmance, appellant's legal counsel must make compelling arguments. More experienced attorneys will presumably be able to draw on that past experience to discern the kinds of arguments that are most likely to be successful. In other words, the more skilled the appellant's counsel, the more able she will be to craft high-quality legal argumentation capable of persuading a reviewing panel to disturb the lower court ruling (Haire, Lindquist, and Hartley 1999). We expect that privately retained, government, and interest group attorneys have, on average, more expertise in this regard. In our sample, a majority of appellants do have the services of private, government or interest group attorneys, but 12 percent of the appellants represented themselves or had a court-appointed attorney. We expect that *pro se* litigants and court-appointed attorneys will have less success persuading the circuit court panel to reverse.

CIRCUIT CHARACTERISTICS. To this point, we have developed hypotheses related to the ideological preferences of the relevant judges, the institutional identities of the circuit judges rendering decisions, and various case characteristics. The last set of factors that shape the decision to reverse the lower court pertains to characteristics of individual circuits: ambiguity of circuit law, norms regarding the permissibility of reversal, and opportunity costs. Let us consider each in turn, beginning with ambiguity. Where the applicable legal principles are ambiguous, district court judges have more difficulty identifying and correctly applying the law. As Susan Haire, Stefanie Lindquist, and Donald Songer explain, "Trial courts . . . face informational deficits that potentially affect the need for and the nature of appellate supervision. In particular, appellate oversight may vary with subordinates' understanding of upper court preferences" (citations omitted; 2003, 153).

Two factors that may cloud legal issues for district court judges are the degree to which circuit decisions are fractured by separate opinions and the size of the circuit. Separate opinions diminish the clarity of the law, "thereby obscuring guidance from the circuit [to the district court] regarding the applicable legal rules" (Hettinger, Lindquist, and Martinek 2003b, 106–7; see also Rowland and Carp 1996; Hellman 1999). This rate of dissent varies across circuits, with the Court of Appeals for the D.C. Circuit having a dissent rate of almost 12 percent and the Court of Appeals for the First Circuit having a dissent rate of 4.5 percent.[9] We lag these dissent rates by one year in our model, under the assumption that judges will be affected by the consistency or inconsistency of signals sent in the recent past, rather than those unfolding during the year in question.[10]

The size of a circuit may also affect district judges' ability to adhere to circuit doctrine, even for those district court judges making every good faith effort to respond to circuit law. The circuits vary in the number of authorized judgeships from three to twenty-eight.[11] The larger the size of the circuit, the more difficult it may be for a district court judge to determine what exactly constitutes compliance with circuit law, since large circuits produce a greater proliferation of precedent (but see Hellman 1999). These considerations give rise to two expectations. First, the higher the dissent rate at the circuit level, the more likely the panel will be to reverse a lower court decision. Additionally, we expect that the larger the circuit, the more likely a panel will be to reverse the lower court.

If ambiguity at the circuit level makes it more difficult for a district court judge to avoid reversible error, caseload considerations and circuit norms structure the opportunities for a reviewing panel to locate and act on reversible error. The deleterious effects of burdensome federal court caseloads have received an enormous amount of attention. Judges themselves, including the chief justice of the United States, have voiced their concerns that the situation has reached a crisis level (e.g., Newman 1993; Reinhardt 1993; Rehnquist 1994). Heavy caseloads are seen as compromising the ability of judges to efficiently process cases and threatening the quality of justice, forcing the courts to turn to various stopgap measures (see Baker 1994). Moreover, heavy workloads might well reduce the likelihood of reversal simply because reversals take more time: first, to identify reversible error, and second, to craft an opinion that provides the necessary guidance for the lower court judge.[12]

The propensity of a circuit to reverse can also diminish (or enhance) the opportunity for lower court reversal. Reversal rates vary considerably across the circuits, suggesting that different circuits may have different norms concerning lower court reversal. In circuits in which the norms regarding lower court reversal are more permissive, the scope of the opportunity for a given panel to reverse a district court ruling is greater. However, where norms mitigate in favor of greater deference to the district court, that scope of opportunity is more circumscribed. We rely on a measure of reversal rate that is lagged by one year.[13]

A Model of Reversing the Lower Court

In the preceding section, we developed an integrated model of the panel decision to reverse, which includes a variety of factors that are likely to influence that decision. We turn next to an examination of court of appeals reversals from 1960 to 1996. To do so, we draw on the Songer Database as our starting point. We limit our analysis to signed opinions decided by three-judge panels.

Approximately 30 percent of the decisions involve what we treat as a full reversal of the lower court decision; that is, the clearest behavioral manifestation of vertical dissensus. This includes decisions that are reversed, reversed and remanded, vacated and remanded, and vacated. A circuit court's treatment of a district court's decision is not necessarily an all or nothing proposition. Panels may simply affirm[14] or reverse a district court ruling,[15] but the courts of appeals are not limited to such a choice. They may, in effect, "split the difference" by affirming in part and reversing in part (or some derivation thereof such as modified, affirmed and modified, affirmed in part and vacated in part). In terms of vertical dissensus, we think of affirming or reversing in full as representing opposite ends of a spectrum, with affirming in part/reversing in part constituting the middle ground between them. An additional 11 percent of the decisions involve this sort of partial reversal; for instance, those that are affirmed in part and reversed or modified in part, with or without remand. The remaining 58 percent affirm the lower court or deny a petition.

It is important to note at the outset that the propensity to reverse varies across both time and circuits. The annual rate of full reversal ranges from just over 3 percent of cases to 60 percent of cases in any circuit in any given year. The Court of Appeals for the Eighth Circuit has the lowest tendency to reverse in full and the lowest variability over time; in that circuit the annual rate ranges from a low of just under 7 percent to a high of more than 33 percent. Contrast this with the Court of Appeals for the Third Circuit, in which the annual reversal rate ranges from a low of 10 percent to a high of 60 percent. Donald Songer, Reginald Sheehan, and Susan Haire (2000) note that, while the dissent rate has increased over time, the rate of reversal across all circuits does not manifest a significant upward trend. This same pattern holds true when examining individual circuits, but with a few exceptions. The Court of Appeals for the Third Circuit had both the highest average rate of reversal and the highest variability in reversal rate over time and also has a substantial upward trend. The First and Seventh Circuits, conversely, have slight downward trends over the thirty-seven-year period, but their downward trends are not nearly as pronounced as the Third Circuit's upward trend.

With this descriptive information in mind, we turn to the results of our model of the likelihood of an affirmance, partial reversal, or full reversal. As noted earlier, these three categories represent an ordered level of agreement—or, more precisely disagreement—with the lower court decision. To assess the relationships between these levels of (dis)agreement and the hypothesized variables, we use an estimation technique called ordered probit. Ordered probit is a common statistical model that is appropriate for situations in which the phenomenon we are interested in—in our case, vertical dissensus—manifests itself in a set of discrete categories that can be ordered in some meaningful way—in our case, affirmance, partial reversal, or full reversal (cf. Long 1997).

The results of the full statistical model appear in the appendix to this chapter. In this section, we identify those factors from our model that demonstrate relationships with reversals that are consistent with our hypotheses. Those factors that do matter according to our statistical model are reported in table 9.

We begin our discussion of our results, however, by noting a factor that did *not* achieve statistical significance. As with horizontal dissensus, we anticipated that ideological disagreement would affect vertical dissensus. In our models of individual judges' choice to dissent, we focused on ideological disagreement between a panel member and the majority opinion writer. In the case of reversal, however, the ideological disagreement of interest is that between the lower district court judge and the three-judge circuit panel. While ideological disagreement influenced an individual circuit judge's decision to dissent, no such relationship emerges in our analysis of the panel decision to reverse the district court judge. In short, our results indicate that ideological disagreement matters within the circuit panel but not across hierarchical levels (i.e., when the disagreement is between the circuit and the district court). Factors other than ideology do, however, structure the likelihood of lower court reversal.

First among these nonideological factors are institutional roles. Recall that, for the chief judge, we identified competing pressures on the propensity to reverse. Specifically, we noted that the chief might be espe-

TABLE 9. Summary of reversal model

VARIABLE	EFFECT
Ideology	
Ideological disagreement	No effect
Institutional roles	
Chief judge as majority opinion writer	Panel *more* likely to reverse
Chief judge on panel	Panel *more* likely to reverse
District court judge as majority opinion writer	Panel *less* likely to reverse
District court judge on panel	No effect
Case factors	
Amicus curiae participation	Panel *more* likely to reverse
Civil rights/liberties claim	Panel *more* likely to reverse
Cross appeals	Panel *more* likely to reverse
Number of issues raised	Panel *less* likely to reverse
Experienced appellant counsel	Panel *more* likely to reverse
Circuit characteristics	
Rate of separate opinions	Panel *more* likely to reverse
Circuit size	No Effect
Reversal rate	Panel *more* likely to reverse
Caseload	No Effect

cially reluctant to reverse a district court judge because of concerns over the potentially deleterious effects of reversal on collegial functioning within the circuit. Alternatively, we suggested that a chief might be more likely to reverse to maintain consistency in circuit doctrine. In subjecting these alternative theoretical explanations to rigorous empirical testing, we find that, when the chief judge of the circuit participates in the decision and acts as the majority opinion writer, the likelihood of a reversal, whether full or partial, increases. Further, when the chief judge of the circuit participates in the decision but is not the majority opinion writer, the effect is quite similar.

The results with regard to the influence of a district court judge sitting by designation are only partially in line with the relationships we initially hypothesized. It is true that the likelihood of a reversal decreases when the district court judge acts as majority opinion writer. Yet, there is no such effect when a district court judge is simply sitting by designation. This difference in results raises interesting questions about the causal mechanism at work. Clearly, the simple presence of a district court judge on a three-judge panel is not sufficient to bring about a greater degree of deference to the lower court. The fact that the panel demonstrates increased deference to the lower court—that is, is less likely to reverse—when a designated judge authors the majority opinion suggests two possible and distinct causal mechanisms. First, a designated judge with control over the opinion may be able to exert influence over the other judges on the panel and thereby secure their acquiescence in deferring to the lower court ruling. Alternatively, designated judges may more frequently be given the opportunity to craft opinions for the majority when the panel has already decided to affirm the lower court.

All of the case characteristics we identified as likely to be related to lower court reversal do, according to our empirical results, manifest an effect. Perplexingly, however, one of these case characteristics—the number of issues raised—demonstrated an influence opposite from our expectations. Instead of a positive relationship between the number of issues raised and the chance the lower court is reversed, we find that the greater the number of issues, the less likely the lower court will be reversed. While we cannot offer any definitive explanations for this result, it may be that complex cases induce district court judges to proceed with extra care, which, ironically, results in fewer reversible errors. Alternatively, the number of issues raised may be associated with the likelihood of reversal, because it signals appellants' efforts to adopt a scattershot approach to their appeals to identify any possible reversible error. This approach is particularly likely in criminal cases, where even apparently frivolous claims are often raised on appeal in an effort to secure reversal of the conviction. Such desperate measures may be more closely associated with less meritorious appeals.

Next, let us consider those case characteristics that proved to be both statistically significant and affect the likelihood of reversal in the way we had expected. First, the presence of an amicus brief on either side increases the probability of a reversal. This finding is consistent with our contention that such a commitment of resources may signal to panel judges the importance of the case and focus their attention even more carefully than usual on the lower court decision, thus making them more sensitive to errors below. The causal mechanism could work in the other direction, of course. Interest groups may be more inclined to file amicus briefs in cases where they perceive the possibility of success on appeal. The presence of a civil rights or civil liberties issue also decreases the probability of an affirmance or, alternatively, increases the probability of a reversal. In sum, the salience of a case matters and matters in such a way that salient cases are more likely to result in lower court reversal. Good news, indeed, for appellants in such cases; not such good news for appellees.

Recall that we argued that cross appeals were likely to be related to reversal, because they reflect a situation in which both parties are displeased by the lower court's decision. Recall, too, that we argued that skilled legal argumentation on behalf of the appellant is reflected by the experience of the legal counsel and in the relationship between counsel and the appellant. Appellants appearing without counsel and those represented by court-appointed, public defender, or legal aid attorneys risk weak arguments as a result of their attorneys' lack of experience, time, or resources. In both instances, our prior expectations were borne out in that both the presence of cross appeals and experienced appellant counsel are associated with lower court reversal.

Next, we consider the impact of those factors that reflect circuit characteristics. Those factors relate to legal ambiguity, circuit norms, and opportunity costs. Only one of our two measures of legal ambiguity holds up to statistical scrutiny. The circuits' propensity to send conflicting messages through separate opinions is clearly associated with a higher reversal rate; circuit size is not. We find that a circuit's propensity to reverse in the previous year is positively related to the probability of a reversal in a given case. In the case of opportunity costs, which we equated with workload, there is no evidence that workload matters either in increasing or decreasing the likelihood of a three-judge panel reversing a district court ruling.

In the discussion above, we have provided a substantive interpretation of the results from our estimation of the statistical model, identifying which variables have an influence on the decision to reverse and whether those variables enhance or diminish the likelihood the panel will reverse the lower court. In this section, we offer further interpretation of the statistical results, this time with an emphasis on providing a sense of the magnitude of the effects. As we did in chapter 3, we first establish baseline probabilities of an affirmance, partial reversal, and full reversal by holding all variables at their mean or mode.[16] Those probabilities appear in the first row of table 10. The baseline probability of an affirmance is 0.608, whereas the baseline probability of a partial reversal is 0.120, and the baseline probability of a full reversal is 0.272. In other words, on average, in 60 percent of the cases, the decision is affirmed in full. Considering both partial and full reversal to indicate at least some level of disagreement between the circuit and district courts in the remaining 40 percent of cases, there is some expression of vertical dissensus. The remaining rows of table 10 illustrate the change in the respective probabilities for affirmance, partial reversal, and full reversal based on changes in the values of different explanatory variables.

TABLE 10. Predicted probabilities for treatment of lower court decision

	PROBABILITY OF AFFIRMANCE	PROBABILITY OF PARTIAL REVERSAL	PROBABILITY OF FULL REVERSAL
Baseline	0.608	0.120	0.272
Chief judge is majority opinion writer	0.558	0.126	0.316
Chief judge is on panel	0.575	0.124	0.301
District judge is majority opinion writer	0.687	0.107	0.206
Presence of amicus curiae brief	0.514	0.130	0.356
Civil rights/liberties issue	0.510	0.130	0.360
Presence of cross appeal	0.541	0.128	0.331
Minimum number of issues (0)	0.567	0.125	0.308
Maximum number of issues (7)	0.731	0.098	0.171
Inexperienced counsel for appellant	0.643	0.115	0.242
Minimum rate of separate opinions (0.019)	0.643	0.115	0.242
Maximum rate of separate opinions (0.409)	0.515	0.130	0.355
Minimum of reversal norm (3.333)	0.670	0.110	0.220
Maximum of reversal norm (60)	0.520	0.129	0.351

To begin with, when the chief judge of the circuit writes the majority opinion, the chance of affirmance decreases by 8 percent, with a concomitant increase in the probability of a full reversal of about 16 percent. The magnitude of the effect of the chief judge is slightly more muted when the chief judge is merely a member of the three-judge panel but not the majority opinion writer, with the likelihood of full affirmance dropping by only a little over 5 percent and the likelihood of full reversal rising by 11 percent. The influence of a district court judge as the majority opinion writer is more substantial in comparison, with the likelihood of affirmance increasing by almost 13 percent.

When we consider the substantive effect of the presence of amicus curiae, we find that it is even more influential, in relative terms, than the effect of either the chief judge or a district court judge as the majority opinion writer. Indeed, when there is amicus curiae participation—regardless of whether it is in support of the appellant, the appellee, or both—the likelihood of affirmance decreases by over 15 percent and the likelihood of full reversal increases by over 30 percent! The effects with regard to the presence of a civil rights or civil liberties claim are similar in this regard.

Cross appeals, which are markers for case complexity, and inexperienced appellant's counsel, an indicator of the quality of legal argumentation, have notable substantive effects as well. Consider, first, the presence of cross appeals. When cross appeals are present, the probability of affirmance is 0.541, compared to 0.608 in the absence of cross appeals. The probability of full reversal, conversely, is 0.331 when there are cross appeals and 0.272 when there are not. In other words, cross appeals result in a decrease in the probability of affirmance of 11 percent and an increase in the probability of full reversal of over 20 percent. With regard to inexperienced counsel, the percentage change in the probability of full affirmance and full reversal are positive 5.8 percent and negative 11 percent, respectively.

Up to this point in our discussion of changes in the probabilities of affirmance and (full) reversal, the variables under discussion have all been discrete variables. In other words, either the condition was or was not present; for example, the chief judge did or did not author the majority opinion, there either was or was not amicus curiae present. Two of the more interesting variables, however, are continuous rather than discrete in nature: the rate of separate opinions and the rate of lower court reversal. Recall that we conceptualized the rate of separate opinions as a measure of legal ambiguity in that the more fractured the circuit's rulings, the more difficult it is for a district court judge to extract guidance from the circuit's body of case law. The rate of lower court reversal, however, is intended to capture circuit norms about the acceptability of lower court reversal. The baseline of separate opinions used to calculate the probabilities for table 10 was 13 percent. Separate opinion rates across circuits and years vary from 0.02 to 0.41. As we move from the minimum observed rate of separate opinions to the maximum rate, the probability of an affirmance drops nearly 0.13, while the probability of full reversal increases by more than 0.11. When we consider the norm of reversal, the percentage of cases with reversal in the prior year ranges from approximately three to sixty. Over this same range, the probability of a full reversal increases from 0.22 to 0.35.

Finally, we turn to two examples with which to examine the likelihood of a reversal. In the first example, we set many of the variables at values that would minimize the probability of a reversal. In the second example, we set the variables at values that would maximize the probability of a reversal. These values are realistic values in that they result from values observed in the data set.

In the first example, the values for the lagged rate of separate opinions and the lagged rate of reversals come from the Court of Appeals for the Fifth Circuit in 1974. The rate of separate opinions was low, less than 2 percent in the previous year. The rate of reversals was also low, only 3.3 percent. In this example, we assume that a district court judge wrote the majority opinion and that the case does not involve a civil rights or a civil liberties claim or amicus curiae participation. Further, we assume that the appellant's counsel was inexperienced and that there are no cross appeals present. This combination of factors leads to predicted probabilities of 0.80 for an affirmance, 0.08 for a partial reversal, and 0.12 for a full reversal. In other words, when conditions are least favorable for appellants seeking reversal, they have only slightly better than a one in ten chance of securing victory. We derive similarly grim predicted probabilities for appellants in other circuits and in other years. For example, appellants with similar case characteristics would have faced similar conditions in the Eighth Circuit in the late 1960s, and thus faced similarly low prospects of obtaining a reversal.

The expected outlook for an appellant is much brighter in other circuits under different circumstances. The Court of Appeals for the D.C. Circuit in the 1970s had rather high historical reversal rates. In addition, the D.C. Circuit also issued separate opinions at a relatively high rate. In 1975, for example, the reversal rate for the Court of Appeals for the D.C. Circuit was almost 57 percent, and the separate opinion rate was 28 percent. Therefore, in 1976, an appellant presenting a case involving a civil rights issue, who was fortunate to have a private attorney and the attention of at least one group that filed an amicus brief, facing a respondent who complicates the issue by filing a cross appeal and finds that the chief judge has written the opinion, would find that the likelihood of a full reversal soars to 0.69 and the likelihood a full affirmance drops to 0.20. This is a remarkable difference compared to our earlier example and illustrates that even a set of less than ideal circumstances can still give an appellant reason for optimism. If we make similar assumptions about the case facts and amicus participation, but we assume that the chief judge is on the panel and that the respondent does not file a cross appeal, we predict that likelihood of a reversal is 0.61. Thus, in this circuit in this period, an appellant's expectations of a reversal are the same as a respondent's baseline expectation of an affirmance for all years in all circuits.

Conclusion

In this chapter, we provided a set of expectations for court of appeals reversal of a lower court decision. Those expectations, like those in chapter 3, reflected an understanding of behavior that is conditioned by ideology, institutional arrangements, and case stimuli. Vertical dissensus, like horizontal dissensus, occurs less often in the U.S. Courts of Appeals than in the U.S. Supreme Court. In the courts of appeals, the presumption favors affirmance, but in the Supreme Court, evidence suggests that the Court grants certiorari in order to reverse (Perry 1991). This difference is most likely a function of the mandatory nature of circuit court dockets.

Our findings further suggest that panel decisions to reverse are not shaped by raw ideological disagreement with the lower court. That is not to say that reversal is based solely on legal factors alone, however. To be sure, some of the variables that demonstrated statistical significance, such as case complexity, may reflect error correction based on legal justifications. In contrast, many of the case and circuit conditions that influence the likelihood of reversal do not support an interpretation suggesting purely legal foundations for affirmance or reversal. For example, unclear signals, third-party intervention, and effective advocacy all influence the likelihood of reversal. While the correction tied to any of these may have a legal foundation, there are other possible explanations. For example, third-party intervention, effective advocacy, and chief participation have more to do with an individual litigant's resources and with circuit management. Another intriguing finding demonstrates the influence of mixed signals on the likelihood of reversal. Specifically, high levels of dissent at the circuit court level complicate the legal resolution of cases for a district court judge, because information regarding appropriate circuit precedent may be confused by conflicting messages. What makes this finding particularly interesting is that, while this noise creates legal ambiguity for a lower court judge, it is, in fact, a function of ideological forces at the circuit level, as we demonstrated in chapters 3 and 4.

Appendix

TABLE 11. Ordered probit model of reversing in full, reversing in part, or affirming

INDEPENDENT VARIABLE	COEFFICIENT	ROBUST STANDARD ERROR
Ideology		
Ideological difference (maj. opinion writer to district court judge) (+)	−0.007	0.058
Institutional roles		
Chief judge maj. opinion writer (−/+)	0.128	0.063*
Chief judge on panel (−/+)	0.084	0.043*
Designated district court judge maj. opinion writer (−)	−0.216	0.069**
Designated district court judge on panel (−)	0.023	0.039
Case factors		
Amicus curiae participation (+)	0.237	0.071***
Civil rights/liberties claim (+)	0.249	0.041***
Cross appeals (+)	0.169	0.055**
Number of issues raised (+)	−0.064	0.014***
Experienced counsel (+)	0.095	0.055*
Circuit characteristics		
Separate opinion rate (+)	0.842	0.321**
Circuit size (+)	0.005	0.004
Reversal rate (+)	0.007	0.002***
Caseload (−)	0.0001	0.0004
μ_1	0.635	0.101
μ_2	0.969	0.101

NOTE: N = 6860; log likelihood = −6291.82.53; Wald $\chi^2_{(14)}$ = 169.49. Robust standard errors cluster on circuit year. * $p < 0.05$, ** $p < 0.01$, *** $p < 0.001$ (one-tailed tests where directionality hypothesized).

TABLE 12. Descriptive statistics for variables in the ordered probit model of panel reversal of lower court

VARIABLE	MEAN	STANDARD DEVIATION	MINIMUM	MAXIMUM
Ordered reversal	0.728	0.898	0	2
Ideological difference	0.351	0.295	0	1.14
Chief judge maj. opinion writer	0.081	0.273	0	1
Chief judge on panel	0.164	0.370	0	1
Designated district court judge maj. opinion writer	0.071	0.257	0	1
Designated district court judge on panel	0.194	0.395	0	1
Amicus curiae participation	0.042	0.201	0	1
Civil rights/liberties claim	0.157	0.364	0	1
Cross appeals	0.061	0.239	0	1
Number of issues raised	1.634	1.197	0	7
Counsel experience	0.879	0.326	0	1
Separate opinion rate	0.131	0.063	0.019	0.409
Circuit size	11.28	4.956	3	28
Reversal rate	27.64	10.62	3.33	60
Caseload	104.04	45.37	25.88	271.25

N = 6860

Conclusions

Judicial Dissensus, Judicial Discretion, and the Institutional Context

This book originated as an effort to understand judicial dissensus, both among judges at the same level of the judiciary (horizontal dissensus) and between judges operating at different levels (vertical dissensus). Although our focus was, first, on the U.S. Courts of Appeals and, then, on the relationship between the U.S. Courts of Appeals and the U.S. District Courts, what we have uncovered with regard to dissensus on and between these courts is important not only for what it tells us about those courts but also for what it illuminates about judicial dissensus more broadly.

We began this line of inquiry drawing on the lessons of the existing theoretical and empirical work on both separate opinions and the reversal of lower courts. These theoretical foundations drew on the major approaches framing the study of judicial behavior, including elements related to judicial attitudes and roles, case characteristics, institutional effects, and strategic considerations. In exploring the empirical dynamics of dissensus on the U.S. Courts of Appeals, some of what we found was entirely consistent with that extant body of work, but some of what we found was more surprising. In these concluding observations, we consider our findings in a broader perspective, paying special attention to the implications of our results for enduring questions concerning legal predictability and stability, for understanding the nature of judicial preferences and behavior on collegial courts, and for illuminating conflicts over values and the resolution of such conflicts in appellate courts.

It is hard to imagine how the importance of understanding horizontal and vertical dissensus among judges could be overstated. Even the implications of horizontal and vertical dissensus are hotly debated. In a positive light, dissensus in the form of separate opinions can ensure that the product of judicial deliberations has been carefully considered, that is, poked and prodded and generally scrutinized by sympathetic and hostile actors alike. Likewise, dissensus in the form of reversal of a lower court promotes the idea that the appellate process serves as a safeguard against aberrant behavior on the part of lower court judges. But, from a less sanguine perspective, both variants of dissensus provide evidence that legal rules are indeterminate in many cases and that judges exercise considerable discretion in applying the law (cf. Songer 1982). Oliver Wendell Holmes's famous definition of law as "the prophecies of what the courts do in fact, and nothing more pretentious" reflects the idea that law is indeterminate with respect to any legal dispute until a judge announces the governing legal principles (1897, 461). Horizontal and vertical dissensus seem to prove Holmes's point.

Because separate opinions and reversals constitute behavioral manifestations of judges' discretionary authority, studies of dissensus shed light on critical questions related to the effective functioning and legitimacy of our legal system and the operation of the rule of law. Typically, the debate over judicial discretion has centered on whether judging is a political enterprise undifferentiated from other forms of lawmaking, or whether judges—because of shared norms, logical analysis, or some other legal constraints—engage in a form of reasoning that provides for some measure of "bounded objectivity" (see Hutchinson 1989). Our findings cut both ways. The evidence we have presented in the preceding pages of this book demonstrates that judging is both a legal and a political activity and that, in either case, it is an activity that takes place in an institutional context that substantially shapes the enterprise.

Horizontal Dissensus

In the data we analyzed, the rate of separate opinions on the U.S. Courts of Appeals is low, averaging about 13 percent across the years we studied but with substantial variation across the circuits (ranging from 2 to 41 percent).[1] Thus, on average, only in a small percentage of cases are judges sufficiently motivated to express their disagreement with the majority, but there is substantial variation. How willing a judge is to issue a separate opinion is likely a function of how strongly she feels about the issue at hand. As Richard Posner has noted, "In a three judge panel, provided that at least one judge has a strong opinion on the proper outcome of the case . . . the other judges, if not terribly interested in the case, may simply cast their vote with the 'opinionated' judge" (1995, 123). As long as one indifferent judge goes along with the opinionated judge, the third must also or otherwise be forced to write a dissenting opinion. When they do dissent, courts of appeals judges do so most often in (1) situations where their preferences deviate from those of the majority opinion writer, (2) ambiguous or salient cases, and (3) circuits where such dissensus is normatively acceptable. Conversely, judges dissent less often when (1) their institutional roles reduce their preference for dissensus and (2) they enjoy a degree of greater prestige.

One of our most robust findings is the effect of attitudes on horizontal dissensus. Greater ideological disagreement within a panel predicts not only dissenting opinions, but also concurring opinions, the implications of which we discuss below. Additionally, ideological disagreement continues to perform well as a predictor of dissent when contrasted with strategic explanations of dissenting behavior. This finding reinforces years of scholarly research, emphasizing that the identities of judges—or, perhaps more accurately, the preferences of those with the responsibility for staffing the bench—play a critical role in shaping judicial outcomes.[2]

After controlling for ideological differences between judges, other factors that condition the decision to dissent have interesting implications for how conflicts are resolved in our legal system. Of special note among these findings is the important influence of circuit-level norms on dissenting behavior. Like many of the most interesting influences on behavior, norms are generally assumed to influence behavior, but they are difficult to measure empirically. Dissent rates, however, are behavioral manifestations of decision-making norms operative at the circuit court level. As noted above, the circuits are certainly not monolithic in their tolerance for dissent. Significantly, these variations in dissent rates (read: variations in norms) help structure the decision of an individual circuit judge to concur or dissent. Institutional context thus has a substantial impact on the likelihood that judges will express their disagreements in the form of dissenting opinions.

How does institutional context affect dissensus on appellate courts? Previous research has debated whether low dissent rates reflect actual consensus or a reluctance to engage in the formal expression of dissensus

(Goldman 1966, 1969; Richardson and Vines 1967; Atkins and Green 1976; Songer 1982). Our finding that circuit norms matter, even after controlling for ideological differences, suggests that suppression—in the sense that some judges might choose *not* to dissent for reasons related to collegiality or norms, even when they may disagree with the majority opinion at some level—may operate in some, and perhaps all, circuits. Other scholars have suggested that time limitations affect judges' inclination to issue separate opinions. Even the most conscientious judge no doubt values his "free" time, whether that time is spent in pursuit of personal leisure or professional activities off the bench (Macey 1997; Posner 1997).[3]

As Klein has observed: "Most people value leisure time, and there is little reason to think judges are different" (2002, 17). Separate opinion authorship, with its attendant consumption of time and energy, obviously translates into less time for other activities. Nevertheless, our findings run contrary to the expectations we derived based on these observations. First, workload differences exhibited no relationship to the likelihood of a separate opinion. Second, one of the independent variables in our horizontal dissensus model that could be interpreted either as a workload indicator or as a collegiality indicator performs in a way that suggests it has more to do with collegiality. Freshman judges are less likely to dissent but statistically are no different than their peers with regard to concurrences. If freshman judges were simply succumbing to workload pressures, we would see fewer concurrences as well. That we only see a reduced dissent rate suggests that collegiality, rather than workload, influences this behavior.

Work by Klein suggests that at least some judges care about efficient case processing because they believe that prompt resolution of cases is important for fairness in the adjudicative process (2002, 25–26). To the extent this is an operative goal for judges, they may well see separate opinion authorship as compromising the achievement of that goal. One judge likely to have a special concern for efficient case processing is the chief judge. Yet we find that, while chief judges are less likely to dissent, they are no less likely to concur. Unless concurrences simply take less time to prepare than dissents, this finding suggests an enhanced concern for collegiality over efficient case processing. This by no means contradicts the suggestion that some judges care about efficient case processing; chief judges themselves may be very concerned about prompt case dispositions at the circuit level. But chiefs are nevertheless just as willing to complicate the decision-making process through concurrences as any other judge.

A final explanation is that judges on the courts of appeals simply care about collegiality and act accordingly. Though a carefully couched separate opinion need not directly challenge collegiality, dissents certainly have the potential to do so, and to a greater degree than concurrences. Hence, a commitment on the part of judges to a norm of collegial relations can serve to suppress the expression of dissents. Although the empirical analyses contained in this book cannot offer definitive evidence on this point, our findings regarding the effect of separate opinion rates on the individual expression of horizontal dissensus suggests that circuit-level norms affect individual-level behavior.

The previous two paragraphs draw attention to the differential findings for chief judges and freshman judges with regard to concurrences and dissents. The differences between the two types of separate opinions suggest to us that these differences are a function of concerns for collegiality more than they are a function of concerns over caseload processing or acclimation pressures. Further, existing scholarship, both classic and contemporary, provides evidence that judges value collegiality. For example, Howard's work included extensive interviews with judges in the D.C., Second, and Fifth Circuits. The commentary offered by the interviewed judges made clear that collegial relations were highly valued (1981, 203–10). More recent work by Jonathan Cohen is also illuminating in this regard. In his extensive interviews with appellate judges and their clerks in the D.C., Seventh, and Ninth Circuits, Cohen, too, found evidence that judges care, and care deeply, about collegial relations among judges (2002, 154–59 and 172–74).

In general, our findings are congruent with those concerning state courts of last resort and the U.S. Supreme Court, with one important exception. Scholars who have devoted time and effort to studying separate opinion authorship in those courts have consistently found that supreme court justices in the state and federal systems use separate opinions as strategic tools. Based on their research, Paul Brace and Melinda Gann Hall averred that understanding judicial choice—including the decision to dissent—requires understanding its strategic underpinnings (1993, 930). Paul Wahlbeck, James Spriggs, and Forrest Maltzman (1999; see also Maltzman, Spriggs, and Wahlbeck 2000) make the same assertion regarding separate opinions in the U.S. Supreme Court.

In contrast, we were unable to find evidence of strategic behavior on the part of dissenting judges on the U.S. Courts of Appeals. Although we carefully constructed a model of the decision to dissent that was explicitly tied to the considerations in which a strategic judge would engage, when subjected to empirical verification, our strategic model failed. Attitudinal theorists may not be surprised at our finding that the strategic account of separate opinion authorship does not travel well to the courts of appeals. Other scholars, however, will no doubt find this result intriguing.

Our findings with respect to strategy and separate opinion authorship are not, by any means, intended as an indictment of the ascendance of strategic models in behavioral scholarship on the courts. The U.S. Courts of Appeals are but one of many American courts and, for some very good reasons, might be among the least likely in which to find evidence of strategic behavior. Strategic calculations require the expenditure of time and intellectual energy. Because of their service as jurists in the appellate workhorses of the federal system, courts of appeals judges may often find themselves in short supply of these resources.

Relatedly, while U.S. Supreme Court or state supreme court justices virtually always dispose of cases with a stable set of colleagues in an *en banc* format, circuit court judges operate in an entirely different decision-making milieu. The rotating three-judge panel format means that circuit court judges face an informational hurdle (about their colleagues' and superiors' preferences, about their colleagues' and superiors' likely reactions) that makes strategic calculations more complicated for them as compared to justices on the federal or state supreme court bench. This is not to suggest that circuit court judges lack the acuity of supreme court justices to engage in strategic calculations; it is not the intellectual capabilities of circuit court judges but the institutional situation in which they find themselves that compromises the ability of circuit court judges to do so.

There is another reason that, while our findings may give pause to strategic theorists, they do not undermine the strategic paradigm in general. Judicial behavior encompasses a broad range of activities, of which separate opinion authorship is but one variety. Although the sentiment embodied in a separate opinion, even a dissent, may be transformed at some future date from the expression of individual disagreement into the articulation of majoritarian precedent, neither a concurrence nor a dissent represents the *sin qua non* of judicial behavior. Arguably, the most fundamental form of judicial behavior is the judicial vote. However, if the content of the majority opinion has the greatest import over the long term, as some have argued (cf. Spriggs 2003), then that opinion (and the process by which it is assigned) is equally consequential as the authoring of dissenting or concurring opinions. It is worth noting, therefore, that circuit judges may undertake strategic calculations with respect to other dimensions or elements of the decision-making process. That being said, it remains a notable finding that the strategic account fails to explain separate opinions in the U.S. Courts of Appeals.

Although we have emphasized some of the differences between our findings for concurrences and dissents in the discussion above, some additional discussion of our findings regarding concurrences is warranted. Although concurrences are more "consensual" in nature than dissents, concurrences still reflect distinct differences of opinion that are often ideologically motivated. Thus, *the content* of the majority opinion—which may have critical implications for future legal relations between the direct parties to the case as well as future litigants—is subject to ideological disagreement no less than the actual case outcome. In a recent essay, James Spriggs noted the importance of judicial preferences for substantive policy as well as case dispositions, concluding in the context of the U.S. Supreme Court that "[i]t is the legal rule announced in an opinion (not which party won the case) that ultimately serves as referents for behavior and alters the perceived costs and benefits decision makers attach to alternative courses of action" (2003, 23). The fact that concurrences, like dissents, are influenced by judicial ideology indicates that it is possible to separate case disposition from substantive policy, even when judges' views of both are based on their attitudes and policy preferences.

What are the implications of our findings with regard to horizontal dissensus for questions of legal indeterminacy and instability? First, legal "indeterminacy" and "stability" are terms that denote the degree to which law is predictable. Where legal outcomes are unpredictable, it may result from the indeterminacy of legal rules or decision uncertainty by adjudicating tribunals (see Priest and Klein 1984; Hanssen 1999). Horizontal dissensus is a *reflection* of the indeterminacy of legal rules, in the sense that judges' disagreements over case outcomes (in the case of dissent) or the rationale used to reach those outcomes (in the case of concurrences) indicate that the applicable legal rules provide different judges with sufficient leeway to choose alternative outcomes even when faced with the same factual scenario. When political scientists discuss nonunanimous decisions, an "objective indicator that legitimate decisional alternatives [are] open to the judges" (Songer 1986, 117), they are often referring to such rule indeterminacy.[4] Our empirical models included measures of such rule indeterminacy to test this particular proposition. Legal indeterminacy of this "ambiguous rule" variety has implications for legal predictability if it undermines citizens' abilities to evaluate the lawfulness of their behaviors.

Yet as Mark Tushnet (1996) points out, rule indeterminacy may be completely consistent with a high degree of legal predictability (and thus certain conceptions of "the rule of law") if sitting judges share similar views and values sufficient to promote consensus regarding the meaning of applicable rules at any given time, or if individual judges' decisions are predictable based on their attitudinal orientations. For those who endorse this view, the high degree of unanimity on the U.S. Courts of Appeals may be comforting, because even if it does not necessarily reflect the existence of determinate legal rules, it at least provides some indication that judges often share certain intersubjective understandings about those rules or at least are willing to acquiesce to the majority view in most cases. Conversely, while this view may be comforting, it nevertheless does not address the question of whether outcomes across rotating panels are sufficiently consistent to promote legal predictability (see Hellman 1999). Judges may act consistently (and thus predictably), but they may not act "coherently" across panels (cf. Kornhauser and Sager 1989).

The discussion above (as well as our empirical analyses) views horizontal dissensus as a dependent variable influenced by the existence of indeterminate rules or shared judicial values. Perhaps more interesting at this point, however, is to consider dissensus as an independent variable. If dissensus is at least one indicator of legal predictability, does dissensus affect behavior outside the courts by affecting citizens' understandings of their legal rights and obligations? Certainly, anecdotal evidence suggests that influential dissents in certain cases (such as *Plessy v. Ferguson*) may help fuel social movements that press for legal change. But would systematic evaluation of dissent rates across courts in different jurisdictions indicate that high levels of dissent produce higher litigation rates or rates of appeal? Future research might explore the extent to which horizontal dissensus affects legal mobilization or lawyers' and citizens' views regarding the predictability of case outcomes (cf. Epp 1990; Hanssen 1999).

Horizontal dissensus thus emerges when the law's constraints are sufficiently loosened through ambiguity to allow the exercise of judicial discretion. By this account, dissents will be more likely in cases where the applicable law is ambiguous, because such ambiguity allows greater room for the exercise of attitudinally based, rather than legally based, judgments. Although we do find that some measures of legal ambiguity help to predict horizontal dissensus, the influence of norms and judge characteristics on the expression of dissensus suggests that the formal expression of disagreement among judges is a sociological and political phenomenon as much as it is a behavioral manifestation of legal ambiguity. The strength of our findings with regard to political and institutional factors indicates that the U.S. Courts of Appeals serve not only to settle conflict, but also to shape the landscape of future conflict through choices based on factors other than the law.

Vertical Dissensus

At the outset of these concluding observations, we noted the enduring debate over whether judging is simply a political exercise or whether judges engage in a form of "bounded objectivity." In assessing whether separate opinions were attitudinally motivated on the courts of appeals, we focused on the extent to which panel members' attitudes were congruent or divergent. In assessing influences on a panel decision to reverse, our focus shifted to the consistency between a reviewing panel's ideological orientation and the attitudes of the district court judge who rendered the judgment below. Comparing the two analyses, we found that attitudinal factors were influential in the case of horizontal dissensus but not in the case of vertical dissensus. It appears that separate opinion writing is a more "political" activity than reversal, which may better be characterized as reflecting a form of bounded objectivity.

This is a remarkable finding. The scholarship devoted to appellate reversal strongly indicates that the match (or mismatch) of preferences between reviewing judges and those under review matters a great deal. Reversal is, after all, the "most definitive and forceful mechanism for communication of legal policy possessed by a higher court" (Smith 2004, 2). With regard to the U.S. Courts of Appeals specifically, "[a]lthough the power to reverse is exercised relatively infrequently by the circuit courts, it nevertheless serves as a compelling mechanism to shape lower court decision making and to signal the circuit's preferences concerning legal policy" (Haire, Lindquist, and Songer 2003, 144). Hence, to the extent that reversal is a vehicle for the courts of appeals to ensure that district court judges remain true, ideological disagreement between the two reasonably should matter.

The empirical results we presented in chapter 5, however, provide no evidence that such disagreement structures the circuit decision to reverse the district court. Rather, other institutional roles, case characteristics, and circuit traits emerged as the important factors for understanding the panel's decision to reverse. In terms of institutional roles, recall that the presence of both chief judges and district court judges sitting by designation on a panel affected the likelihood of reversal, although in opposite ways. The presence of a chief judge, whether simply as a panel member or as the majority opinion writer, increased the likelihood of reversal, while the presence of a designated district court judge reduced that likelihood. With regard to case characteristics, we found panels more likely to reverse when cases are salient, complex, and involve experienced counsel on behalf of the appellant. Ambiguity in the form of mixed signals from the circuit to the district court judges within that circuit and norms regarding the permissibility of lower court reversal also came into play, demonstrating again that institutional context is essential to understanding dissensus.

What, then, should we make of the fact that reversal is not ideological in nature in terms of the compatibility of preferences between circuit court panels and district court judges? This is an especially pressing question in light of the evidence provided by Susan Haire, Stefanie Lindquist, and Donald Songer (2003) in their recent work on reversals of district court judges by circuit court panels. In their study, Haire et al. similarly analyzed ideological disagreement between the two levels, leading them to conclude that "circuit courts tend to reverse decisions below in order to further their own preferences" (2003, 162). The apparent discrepancy between our findings and those of Haire and her colleagues is likely related to differences in the cases examined. While Haire, Lindquist, and Songer focused exclusively on civil rights decisions rendered in the U.S. Courts of Appeals, our analysis casts a broader net to analyze cases covering the gamut of substantive issues handled by these courts. Thus, it may be the case that ideological considerations do not manifest themselves in the decision of a panel to reverse a district court except under specialized conditions, namely when the case involved is highly charged in terms of ideological content.

Further, our finding that, in general, ideological differences between "reviewers" and "reviewees" are not significantly related to reversal suggests that reversal often involves error correction in a technical sense rather than error correction in the form of supervisory policymaking. As Burton Atkins has observed, "An appellate court's basic contribution is error correction" (1990, 74). Where error correction dominates the reversal decision—which may involve technicalities of trial procedure or practice that are arguably nonideological in nature—ideology is less important to the reviewing court's judgment. We note, however, that this oft-cited distinction between technical error correction and policy correction is not self-evident. Distinguishing between cases that raise technical as opposed to policy questions on appeal may often be difficult. For example, in the *Reid-Walen* case cited in chapter 1, the appellate court reversed on the issue of whether Missouri was a *forum non conveniens*. At first glance, this may appear to constitute a technical matter involving trial logistics and convenience. Yet, at another level, the appellate court's decision—and the creation of precedent in the area—has potentially significant implications for the feasibility of plaintiffs' tort suits, an area that has become ideologically charged in recent years. Perhaps it is no surprise that Judge William H. Timbers (a Republican appointee) supported the dismissal of the plaintiffs' suit via his dissenting opinion, while Chief Judge Donald Lay (a Democratic appointee), writing for the panel majority, allowed the suit to go forward. Future research focused on the continued utility of the distinction between error correction in a technical sense and error correction in a policy sense would provide valuable insights into the decision making of appellate judges.

In terms of circuit traits, of particular note is our finding regarding reversal norms. In his study of appellate interventions in the U.S. Courts of Appeals, Atkins (1990) recognized the power of legal culture to shape intervention rates. Here we observe the same phenomenon: reversal is simply more likely in some circuits than in others as a result of predominant norms. Empirically, we demonstrated in chapter 5 that prior reversal rates meaningfully shape the likelihood that a panel will reverse the lower court. In other words, as we found with the expression of horizontal dissensus, we found norms are consequential in structuring the expression of vertical dissensus.

Comparing Horizontal and Vertical Dissensus

The primary difference between vertical and horizontal dissensus we uncovered involves the influence of attitudes, as noted above. The decision of a court of appeals jurist to file a concurring or dissenting opinion is fundamentally related to the expression of attitudinal disagreement between that judge and her brethren on the panel. In contrast, ideological disagreement between a circuit panel and the district court judge below does not structure panel decisions to reverse the lower court. Observers of the judicial hierarchy concerned with notions of judicial objectivity may find this result satisfying, as it is more consistent with the idea of a "bounded objectivity" than with the idea of judging as a vehicle for the pursuit of ideological goals. For participants in the judicial hierarchy, particularly litigants, this may also come as welcome news; while judges may indulge their ideological orientations when writing separate opinions (which have no direct or immediate impact on winners or losers in the instant case), such ideologically motivated behavior is less prevalent with regard to the choice to reverse.

We do not wish to overstate this distinction: both reversals and dissenting opinions involve the question of whether the appellant or the appellee should prevail. There is an important difference, however, in the nature of these judicial acts. The choice to write a separate opinion is individualistic. Certainly justices on the U.S. Supreme Court can find themselves dissenting or concurring alone. But, because the justices hear cases and render decisions as a group, a justice contemplating a concurrence or dissent can (usually) find a like-minded compatriot to join his separate opinion. Accordingly, the size of court is related to the rate of dissent on state supreme courts, because judges may find "strength in numbers" and a greater willingness to dissent when others participate in the dissent as well (see Sheldon 1999, 120).

The fact that the U.S. Courts of Appeals decide cases predominately with the use of three-judge panels means, by definition, that a separate opinion author will never be joined by a colleague, because to do so would be to create a new majority. In the case of the U.S. Courts of Appeals, it should therefore not be surprising that these decisions are dominated by individual judges' attitudes. As Justice Charles Hughes remarked, "Dissenting opinions enable a judge to express his individuality. He is not under compulsion of speaking for the court and thus securing the concurrence of a majority. In dissenting, he is a free lance" (Hughes quoted in Sheldon 1999, 133 n.7).

A reversal, however, requires something akin to a team effort. The fact that reversal is rendered by a panel rather than an individual judge—that is, it is collegial in the sense of being a decision vested in a group of ostensibly coequal colleagues—means that the influence of collegiality may explain why attitudinal disagreement between circuit panels and district judges fails to affect appellate intervention in any systematic fashion. In this regard, our analysis presents a slightly different perspective on appellate hierarchy than is typically portrayed in the literature. Most political scientists conceive of the appellate hierarchy as promoting a principal-agent relationship between "a small set of politically dominant judges [seeking] to enforce their views on recalcitrant judges lower in the hierarchy" (Kornhauser 1999, 46; for examples, see Songer, Segal, and Cameron 1994; Benesh 2002; Haire, Lindquist, and Songer 2003). Lewis Kornhauser (1999) presents an alternative theory of hierarchical court organization that he calls the "team model." According to this theory, appellate judges share the common objective of maximizing the number of "correct" decisions with the primary goal of error minimization through appellate review. This theory supports the notion that appellate panels focus more on institutional efficacy rather than attitudinal or ideological outcomes consistent with judicial preferences (see also Klein 2002, 25–26). Seen in this light, our findings are more consistent with a team model rather than a principal-agent model of appellate review.

Although we find no evidence that attitudinal disagreement between a panel and district court judge affects the panel decision to reverse the lower court, attitudinal disagreement of another kind does matter. Specifically, attitudinal disagreement among judges serving in a circuit that manifests itself in the prevalence of separate opinions results in ambiguous or conflicting guidance from the circuit court to the district courts. The ultimate consequence is more frequent reversals of the district court. Hence, as an institutional act, reversal is not driven by attitudinal disagreement between levels of courts, but attitudinal disagreement among circuit court judges in the aggregate does enhance the frequency with which the institutional act of reversal occurs. In this sense, our findings document "the contagion of conflict" described by Atkins, as horizontal dissensus is important for understanding vertical dissensus. This "contagion of conflict" may extend outside the court system as well. Like horizontal dissensus, vertical dissensus carries implications for legal predictability and stability.

Reversals "have significance beyond the immediate case, because they transmit cues to other litigants, real and potential, about the possible worth of using appellate intervention for their own benefit in the future" (Atkins 1990, 99). Once again, circuit court judges settle conflict for the participants to the immediate case, but they also shape the rules governing struggles over the lines demarcating our shared legal values. This makes understanding how patterns of reversal affect litigation rates and the propensity to appeal even more important.

According to one prominent treatise on jurisprudence: "An understanding of the judicial process . . . requires cognition of [the] institutional nexus of conduct. Every institution embodies some degree of consensus about how it is to operate" (Freeman 1994, 1257). As discussed above, our empirical findings highlight the accuracy of this observation. With respect to vertical dissensus, institutional factors and objectives appear to dominate circuit judges' decision-making calculus, with judges' ideological predispositions moderated by their collegial decision-making environment. In the case of horizontal dissensus, judges do act in a relatively solitary and ideological manner. Yet even the choice to dissent is sometimes moderated by institutional constraints and concerns for collegiality.

These conclusions reinforce the idea that the behavior of political actors (including judges) cannot be viewed in isolation from the institutional context, which profoundly shapes the actors' expectations and understandings of appropriate behavior. Judges, like all human beings, may be motivated to achieve their own personal objectives, but they are simultaneously affected in a substantial way by their colleagues' expectations as well. At least on the federal courts of appeals, however, individual judges' expectations regarding other judges' actions and beliefs do not necessarily promote strategic behavior, at least in terms of dissenting opinions. Rather, circuit judges' responsiveness to institutional context promotes consensus. The portrait of judges painted here, then, is not of isolated actors strategically calculating how best to use institutional constraints to their advantage, but rather of sociologically and institutionally embedded actors whose behavior is responsive to their environment and to their colleagues on the bench. The U.S. Courts of Appeals may be political institutions, but they are institutions first and foremost, and the "institutional nexus of conduct" profoundly shapes individual-level behavior within these courts.

APPENDIX

Data
and
Methods

The U.S. Courts of Appeals Database was funded by the National Science Foundation (SES-8912678). The database includes a sample of cases from each circuit for each year from 1925 to 1988. A later phase of the project added the years 1989 to 1996. These data provided the foundation for our research. We used data from the years 1960 to 1996 in chapters 3 and 5 and data from the years 1971 to 1996 in chapter 4. We restricted the cases in our analyses to decisions involving three-judge panels and those with signed opinions only. In the chapters on dissent and concurrence, the individual judge's decision in each case serves as the unit of analysis, although we excluded the majority opinion writer because she serves as the point of comparison for ideological distance (and since she is assumed to be a part of the majority). This research strategy required converting a single case observation into three observations, one for each judge, and then deleting the observation for the majority opinion writer. In the reversal chapter, the individual case decision served as the unit of analysis; hence, we did not reshape the data to conduct the statistical analysis.

We carefully reviewed the data on a case-by-case basis so as to confirm the presence of a signed opinion and the identity of the majority opinion writer and to clarify any other information about individual cases in the database. We relied at different times on Westlaw, Lexis-Nexis Academic Universe, and the print version of the *Federal Reporter* for this information.

The Multi-User Database on the Attributes of U.S. Appeals Courts Judges 1801–1994 provided important information on the background of the judges and their appointment dates. Each judge in this database shares a unique identifier with the courts of appeals judges in the Courts of Appeals Database, and this allowed us to combine critical information in the two databases. We relied on the Federal Judges Biographical Database provided by the Federal Judicial Center to obtain information on post-1994 appointments. This database also provided the background and appointment information we needed for U.S. District Court judges. With the help of our research assistants, we created a database on these judges that could be merged with the U.S. Courts of Appeals Database, using the unique district court judge identifier in that database.

We employed the ideology measures that Micheal Giles, Virginia Hettinger, and Todd Peppers developed for Courts of Appeals judges (2002). They relied on their own updated version of the attributes database to develop these scores and, thus, the Giles, Hettinger, and Peppers data share the unique identifier system with the other databases. Additionally, Sheldon Goldman shared his collection of American Bar Association ratings for all judicial nominees since President Eisenhower, and we incorporated these data into our expanded background database.

We now turn to the statistical techniques we relied on to conduct our various analyses. First, we note that many of the behaviors of judges and courts are discrete in nature. In the simplest case, we observe either the presence or absence of a particular action. For example, in chapter 4, we investigate the decision of a judge on a U.S. Courts of Appeals panel to file a dissent. In such situations, we observe a dichotomous variable: the judge either files a dissent or votes with the majority. At other times the discrete outcomes that we observe can take on one of a limited set of values. For example, in chapter 5, we examine the decision of a U.S. Court of Appeals panel to affirm the lower court ruling, reverse the lower court ruling, or affirm in part and reverse in part. There are thus three discrete choices available to the panel; we model judges' choices among these options. In both of these examples, the discrete choice (e.g., filing a dissent, reversing the lower court) is the *dependent variable.* We seek to explain judges' choice based on explanatory factors called *independent variables.* The dependent variable is also commonly referred to as Y and the independent variables are referred to as Xs.

Starting with the simplest case—the situation in which our dependent variable is dichotomous—we can think of each observation in terms of the likelihood a judge on the U.S. Courts of Appeals will file a dissenting opinion in that case. In any given case, if we observe the judge casting a dissenting vote, then Y = 1; if not, then Y = 0. Accordingly, one may conceptualize the dependent variable in terms of the probability of observing

Y = 1. If the decision to file a dissenting opinion is entirely random, then half of the time we would expect to see a dissent and half of the time we would not.

Of course, we do not think judges' decisions to dissent are random. We expect (that is, we hypothesize) that the characteristics of the judges involved, the cases themselves, and the circuits in which these decisions are made, influence the likelihood that an individual judge will dissent. These factors are the independent variables that we believe explain a judge's decision to dissent (the dependent variable). We seek to determine whether these independent variables—hypothesized to influence judges' choices to dissent—do, *in fact,* influence the likelihood of a dissent. If they do, we also want to know how much influence they have on that choice. In other words, we evaluate which factors make it more or less likely for us to observe the presence of a dissent as well as how much those factors affect the likelihood of a dissent.

Logit is a statistical estimation tool that lets us evaluate the influence of our independent variables on our dependent variable when the dependent variable is dichotomous, as in the case of a judge's decision whether or not to file a dissent. In doing so, it derives a coefficient, also called a parameter estimate, for each independent variable. These parameter estimates, which are conventionally denoted as β, tell us whether a given independent variable makes it more or less likely that a judge will file a dissenting opinion. If a parameter estimate is positive, then the larger the value of the independent variable, the greater the likelihood of a judge filing a dissent. Conversely, if a parameter estimate is negative, the larger the value of the independent variable, then the smaller the likelihood of a judge filing a dissent. If a parameter estimate is equal to zero, then there is no effect of that variable on the likelihood of a judge filing a dissent.

To see how this works in practice, consider the results we report in table 7 in the appendix to chapter 4. The parameter estimate for ideological disagreement is positive. This means that the greater the ideological disagreement between a judge on a panel and the majority opinion writer, the greater the likelihood of that judge dissenting from the majority opinion. Notice that there are other parameter estimates that are positive. For example, the parameter estimate for Supreme Court enhancement is positive, which suggests that a dissent is more likely when a judge would prefer the outcome if the Supreme Court reviewed the case compared to the outcome represented by the panel decision. But that parameter estimate is so slight in terms of its effect that we can consider it "statistically insignificant."

Evaluating whether a parameter estimate is statistically insignificant is the same as determining whether a parameter estimate is tantamount to equaling zero in a statistical sense. Stated differently, these statistical techniques produce a best guess as to the nature and intensity of the relationship between an independent and dependent variable. The better our best guess is, the more confident we can be in it. To evaluate the quality of our "best guess," we can turn to the standard errors that are associated with each parameter estimate. These standard errors provide the expected range of the parameter estimate. In the case of ideological disagreement, the standard error is 0.261. Statistical theory tells us therefore that we can be 95 percent confident that the true value of the parameter for ideological disagreement falls in the range of ± 1.96 standard errors of our parameter estimate. In the case of ideological disagreement, then, this means we can be 95 percent confident that the true value is 0.782 ± 0.512 (that is, ± 1.96 * 0.261), which makes the value range from 0.270 to 1.294. Notice that this range does not include zero, so we can be 95 percent confident that the true value of the parameter for the effect of ideological disagreement on the likelihood of filing a dissent is not zero.

This is not the case, however, when we consider Supreme Court enhancement. In that case, the parameter estimate is 0.120 and the standard error is 0.797. This means that we can be 95 percent confident that the true value (the true effect of) Supreme Court enhancement on the likelihood of dissent is 0.120 ± 1.56 (that is, ± 1.96 * 0.797), or between −0.360 and 1.68. Notice that this range does include zero. Accordingly, it is possible that the parameter estimate for Supreme Court enhancement is merely an artifact of chance rather than a reflection of the real relationship between Supreme Court enhancement and the likelihood of a judge filing a dissent. So, in this case, the parameter estimate is virtually indistinguishable from zero in a statistical sense.

The situation in the case of phenomena for which we can observe more than two discrete outcomes can be handled using other maximum likelihood techniques. Which technique is appropriate depends on the nature of the set of discrete outcomes we have. Sometimes a set of discrete outcomes can be ordered while other times they cannot. To illustrate, compare our investigation of a U.S. Court of Appeals judge to join the majority, file a concurrence, or file a dissent in chapter 3, with our examination of a U.S. Court of Appeals panel to affirm the lower court, reverse the lower court, or affirm in part and reverse in part the lower court in chapter 5. In the latter case, we can arrange the three choices for a panel based on the level of disagreement a panel has with the lower court, with affirmance representing no disagreement, affirm in part and reverse in part representing partial disagreement, and reversal representing complete disagreement. In the former case, though at first blush it might appear that a concurrence represents a lesser level of disagreement with the majority opinion than a dissent, as we discuss in chapter 3, it is unlikely that this is truly the case. So, while it makes sense to order the possible outcomes when it comes to lower court reversal, it does not make sense to order them in the case of separate opinions. When we can order the set of choices, the dependent variable is said to be ordinal. When we cannot order the set of choices, the dependent variable is said to be nominal.

When the variable of interest is nominal and can take on more than two values, multinomial logit is the appropriate maximum likelihood technique. We can think of multinomial logit as a straightforward extension of the logit technique discussed above. Logit produces a set of parameter estimates that tells us about the likelihood of observing something happening compared to the likelihood of not observing that thing happening. Multinomial logit produces a set of parameter estimates for pairs of outcomes. In chapter 3, we have three possible outcomes (join the majority, dissent, concur). Applying multinomial logit to this situation, we end up with two sets of parameter estimates; one corresponding to the likelihood of concurring rather than joining the majority opinion and one corresponding to the likelihood of dissenting rather than joining the majority opinion.

When it comes to interpreting these sets of parameter coefficients, the logic is the same as with the interpretation of logit parameter estimates. To illustrate, consider the results we report in table 3 in the appendix to chapter 3. The first set of parameter estimates gives us information about the likelihood of concurring relative to the likelihood of joining the majority. The parameter estimate for ideological disagreement (between a judge and the majority opinion writer) is positive (0.551), indicating that the greater the ideological disagreement between the two, the more likely a judge is to concur. The second set of parameter estimates, which provides information about the likelihood of dissenting relative to the likelihood of joining the majority, demonstrates that ideological disagreement is also positively associated with the likelihood of a dissent (0.562), that is, the greater the ideological disagreement between a judge and the majority opinion writer, the greater the likelihood that judge will dissent. As in the case of our logit estimation in chapter 4, we also need to evaluate whether our parameter estimates derived with the help of multinomial logit really indicate that there is a relationship between each independent variable and the dependent variable (as opposed to being the result of chance). Again, we turn to the standard errors, applying the same logic to ascertain whether the standard errors indicate the effect of a variable is statistically indistinguishable from zero or not.

Multinomial logit is not the most appropriate technique when the variable we are investigating is ordinal rather than nominal. Our analysis in chapter 5 of a U.S. Courts of Appeals panel to affirm in full, affirm in part and reverse in part, and reverse in full is, in fact, ordinal. Ordered probit is an appropriate tool for such data. Like logit, ordered probit produces one set of parameter estimates. To illustrate the interpretation of ordered probit estimates, consider those reported in table 11 in the appendix to chapter 5. Consider, as an example, the parameter estimate for amicus curiae participation, which is 0.237. As discussed in greater detail in chapter 5, we hypothesize that amicus curiae participation is an indicator of the salience of a case. Cases that are more salient are likely to receive more scrutiny on appeal, making it more likely for any errors to be identified and thus making reversal more likely. The positive parameter estimate for amicus curiae participation supports this hypothesis. And, just as in the case of logit and multinomial logit, the standard errors give us the information we need to decide if a variable really has an effect on the likelihood of affirming in full, affirming in part and reversing in part, and reversing in full or, alternatively, if the variable's effect is really no different from zero.

NOTES

ONE Horizontal and Vertical Dissensus

1. 315 F.3d 1143 (9th Cir. 2002).
2. 933 F.2d 1390 (11th Cir. 1991).
3. 933 F.2d 1390, 1394 n.4 (8th Cir. 1990).
4. 933 F.2d 1390, 1401 (8th Cir. 1990).
5. The Courts of Appeals were created by the Evarts Act in 1891.
6. The territories of Guam, the Virgin Islands, and the Northern Mariana Islands also each have a district court. While these congressionally created territorial courts have the same federal jurisdiction as other district courts, they are different from the other ninety-one district courts in two important ways. First, they exercise local jurisdiction as well as federal jurisdiction. Second, they are so-called Article I courts, meaning they were created under Congress's Article I authority and judges sitting on these courts do not enjoy the independence protections provided under Article III.
7. The total number of judges serving in a given district court varies over time for two reasons. First, Congress periodically increases the number of permanent district court judgeships. Second, Congress also can and has created temporary judgeships. When Congress creates a temporary judgeship, which may or may not become permanent later on, the judge appointed to that position is still appointed for life and is protected against diminution of salary while in office. If a judgeship is not subsequently made permanent, typically the next vacancy on that district court remains unfilled.
8. The U.S. Court of International Trade and the U.S. Court of Federal Claims are also federal trial courts, but, unlike the U.S. District Courts, these trial courts have very specialized, limited jurisdictions.
9. While the official name is "United States Courts of Appeals," theses courts are colloquially referred to as circuit courts, harkening back to earlier circuit courts, which were abolished in 1912.
10. The Court of Appeals for the Federal Circuit is a specialized court of appeals. Created by Congress in 1982, the U.S. Court of Appeals for the Federal Circuit combined

the jurisdiction of the Court of Custom and Patent Appeals with the appellate jurisdiction of the old Court of Claims. Though it is based in Washington, D.C., the Court of Appeals for the Federal Circuit exercises nationwide jurisdiction.

11. Three-judge panel decisions may be reviewed by all judges within the circuit, which is referred to as an *en banc* hearing. Because it has so many judges, the Ninth Circuit uses a special "mini-*en banc*" procedure, whereby eleven judges, including the chief judge, sit in rotating *en banc* panels (cf. Hellman 2000).

12. Almost all appeals to the U.S. Supreme Court arrive as petitions for a writ of certiorari, literally a request from a litigant for the U.S. Supreme Court to send for and review the lower court record.

13. See table B, Director of the Administrative Office of the U.S. Courts, *Judicial Business of the United States Courts: Annual Report of the Director,* 2002.

14. See table 2-8, Lee Epstein, Jeffrey A. Segal, Harold J. Spaeth, and Thomas G. Walker, *Supreme Court Compendium,* 3rd ed. (Washington, D.C.: CQ Press, 2003).

15. A handful of states actually have two intermediate appellate courts, one to handle criminal appeals and one to handle civil appeals.

16. 78 F.3d 932 (5th Cir. 1996).

17. 539 U.S. 306 (2003).

18. 355 F.3d 697 (D.C. Cir. 2004).

19. Although circuit courts also decide cases *en banc,* in this discussion and generally throughout this book, we focus on decision making by randomly drawn three-judge panels on the U.S. Courts of Appeals.

20. A three-judge panel may actually include two concurring judges who disagree on the proper rationale for the decision. In that case, the "majority" opinion simply refers to the opinion by the judge initially assigned to draft it.

21. From an empirical perspective, there are very few instances in which a judge registers a concurring or dissenting opinion but fails to author a supporting opinion; data from the U.S. Courts of Appeals Database suggests that the frequency is as low as 5 percent of all concurrences and dissents. As Judge Frank Coffin has noted regarding concurrences, "A judge should never merely declare that she concurs" (1994, 227).

22. Roscoe Pound proposed four types of dissent: the rearguard action (defending the old order in changing times), the reconnaissance dissent (which expresses the hope that the majority opinion will be altered in response to changing conditions), the cautious dissent (cautioning against the adaptation of the law to changing conditions too quickly), and the exploratory dissent (discussing existing law as failing to respond to current conditions) (discussed in Peterson 1981, 413).

23. 163 U.S. 537, 559 (1896).

24. Of course, appeals are not the only feasible mechanism for reducing error in this sense. Investing resources to improve adjudication in trial courts could accomplish the same goal. But, as Steven Shavell has asserted, an appeals process is arguably a superior mechanism in that it shifts a substantial proportion of the costs to litigants: "The appeals process . . . may allow society to harness information that litigants have about erroneous decisions and thereby to reduce the incidence of mistake at low cost" (Shavell 1995, 382).

25. As Burton Atkins has noted, "interventions have significance beyond the immediate case, because they transmit cues to other litigants, real and potential, about the pos-

sible worth of using the appellate intervention for their own benefit in the future" (1990, 99).

26. 818 F.2d 97, 106 n.8 (1st Cir. 1987).

27. *Jordan v. Lefevre*, 206 F.3d 196, 199 (2000).

28. See also Thomas Miceli and Metin Coşgel (1994) for a formal model of the influence of reputation on the adoption of legal rules.

29. One potential caveat to note is the desire of an associate justice for elevation to the chief justice position. For example, Justice Robert Jackson was clearly interested in being named chief justice (Gerhart 1958, 235–88).

30. A finding of reversible error by an appellate panel is least likely with regard to a factual determination. "Legal truth, like beauty, is in the eye of the beholder. If there is an evidentiary basis for the judge's interpretation of the facts, this interpretation, unlike interpretations of the law, is virtually immune from appellate review" (District Court judge Constance Baker Motley, quoted in Rowland 1991, 66).

31. Courts of appeals judges themselves have also indicated that the personal values of judges matter in the adjudication process (Friendly 1961; Newman 1984; Edwards 1991).

TWO Theoretical Perspectives on Decision Making in Appellate Courts

1. 531 U.S. 98 (2000).

2. 292 F.3d 597 (9th Cir. 2002).

3. The first congressional codification of the pledge read as follows: "I pledge allegiance to the flag of the United States of America and to the Republic for which it stands, one Nation indivisible, with liberty and justice for all."

4. On June 14, 2004, the Supreme Court reversed the Ninth Circuit decision based on the conclusion of five of the justices that Newdow lacked standing to bring the case (124 S.Ct. 2301).

5. 913 F.Supp. 232, 242 (SDNY 1996).

6. 921 F.Supp. 211 (SDNY 1996). After Judge Baer's ruling reversing his earlier suppression of the evidence seized from the rental car, Carol Bayless sought to have Judge Baer recuse himself from the case. Though the judge declined to do so, he did request that the case be transferred to another district court judge. That judge was Robert P. Patterson Jr., before whom Bayless pled guilty.

7. There is, however, some dispute as to whether Holmes is properly characterized as a realist, since some of his writings sound quite formalistic in nature.

8. Some who are disdainful of this school of thought colorfully characterize legal realism as a theory that predicts a judge's decision based on what he had for breakfast and if he got enough sleep the night before (cf. Kozinski 1993).

9. The Supreme Court's original jurisdiction is limited to suits involving ambassadors and other high-ranking diplomatic personnel, and cases in which a state is a party. Of the Court's original jurisdiction cases, the Court is only required to hear suits between states, with original jurisdiction for the other case categories shared with the U.S. District Courts. It is an exceedingly rare event for the Supreme Court to hear any original jurisdiction case.

10. Three-judge district courts are special panels created on an ad hoc basis to handle a particular case. Created originally as a congressional attempt to rein in the authority

of individual federal court judges to invalidate state actions under the federal Constitution (Solimine 1996, 83–84), three-judge district courts (usually consisting of two district and one circuit court judge) now hear cases dealing with reapportionment and issues involving the Voting Rights Act.

11. Supreme Court justices may be impeached, but this is an exceedingly unlikely event. Only one justice has ever been impeached by the House of Representatives, Samuel Chase in 1804. Chase was impeached but not convicted, as the Senate subsequently acquitted him on all eight articles of impeachment.

12. This was not always the case. For example, John Jay, the first chief justice of the United States, resigned to become the governor of the State of New York and Associate Justice David Davis resigned from the Court to take a seat in the U.S. Senate in 1877. Further, there are a few more recent exceptions, including Arthur J. Goldberg, who stepped down from the Court to assume the U.S. ambassadorship to the United Nations.

13. Indeed, few rigorous empirical studies on the subject exist (Spiller and Gely 1992; Segal 1997; Hettinger 1999) and the bulk of existing research is theoretical rather than empirical in nature (e.g., Gely and Spiller 1990; Eskridge 1991). Some of the empirical evidence available suggests the Court is sensitive to legislative reaction, while other empirical evidence suggests it is not. There is, however, more decisive evidence supporting this thesis in the case of state supreme courts (Langer 2002).

14. Wenner and Dutter explain the relationship between region and ideological values as arising from the "shared historical experiences of people living in the same region" (1988, 115).

15. Chief judges may also ask the chief justice of the Supreme Court for the assistance of district and/or circuit court judges from other circuits. The vast majority of judges serving by designation are, however, district court judges serving as circuit court judges within their own circuits.

16. See table S-3, Director of the Administrative Office of the U.S. Courts, *Judicial Business of the United States Courts: Annual Report of the Director,* various years.

17. The membership of these three-judge panels is determined essentially by lot and then randomly assigned to predetermined blocks of cases. The evidence suggests, however, that this was not always the case. An analysis by Atkins and Zavoina (1974) indicated that Chief Judge Elbert Tuttle of the Court of Appeals for the Fifth Circuit controlled the composition of three-judge panels assigned to hear race relations cases. More recently, charges were levied that Chief Judge Boyce Martin (of the Sixth Circuit) rigged the lineup of judges on the panel that heard *Gratz v. Bollinger,* 539 U.S. 244, and its companion, *Grutter v. Bollinger,* 539 U.S. 306, to ensure more favorable treatment of the University of Michigan Law School and undergraduate admissions affirmative action programs under review.

18. *En banc* rehearing can also come about as a result of calls from a circuit's own judges (Wasby 2002, 183).

19. Rathjen couched his findings in a theory of psychological dissonance in which justices file dissents to satisfy psychological needs, whereas Brenner and Spaeth situated their findings in small group theory.

20. In a regular concurrence, a justice agrees with both the outcome at which the majority arrived and the reasoning used to arrive at that outcome by the majority opinion but wishes to expound on a particular point. In a special concurrence, a justice agrees with the outcome but not the reasoning.

21. Spitzer and Talley (2000) argue that ideological disagreement between a reviewing panel and a lower court judge can increase efficiency for the former. The basic logic is that when there is ideological disagreement between a superior and an inferior, the superior can focus his energies on auditing decisions of the inferior that comport with the ideological preferences of the inferior.

22. The careful work of Brudney and Ditslear (2001) is a notable exception, though their focus is exclusively on labor law. See also Haire, Lindquist, and Songer (2003) and Peppers, O'Harra-Vigilante, and Zorn (2004).

23. Many U.S. Courts of Appeals decisions are rendered without published opinions, and thus the Songer Database is limited in this important respect. Nevertheless, published opinions are generally issued in the more important policymaking cases. For that reason, findings based on the random sample of cases in the Songer Database allow, at the very least, for generalization to the population of policymaking matters before these courts.

THREE Why Do Judges Write Separate Opinions?

1. We start with 1960 for one very practical reason. A key part of the explanation that we explore in this chapter and the following chapter regarding the decision to file a separate opinion, as well as the decision to reverse the lower court (which we investigate in chapter 5), relates to attitudinal disagreement. Because this is such an important factor, it is essential that we have a sound measure of the ideological preferences of the relevant actors. Before 1960, however, very little of the necessary data is available.

2. We did so by reading the text of those decisions, using either Lexis Nexis or Westlaw.

3. The exception to this is the Sixth Circuit. In the Sixth Circuit, majority opinions are assigned on a rotating schedule rather than by the senior (or chief) judge on the panel. In the event that the judge whose turn it is to author the "majority" opinion is not actually in the majority, the opinion he writes becomes his individual dissent.

4. As Maltzman, Spriggs, and Wahlbeck (2000) document (as did Murphy [1964] before them), justices on the Supreme Court are extensively engaged in negotiations and accommodations regarding the content of written opinions. While there is no definitive evidence regarding this phenomenon in the courts of appeals, the heavier workloads faced by circuit judges suggest that negotiations of this kind are less extensive.

5. An illustrative sampling of the most recent of this scholarship includes Bell (2002a, 2002b); Binder and Maltzman (2002); and Massie, Hansford, and Songer (2004). Arguably, the seminal work in this regard, however, is Goldman (1997).

6. These scores were derived from earlier work by Poole and Rosenthal (1997), in which the authors developed measures of congressional preferences based on voting behavior. Because these measures were comparable across both chambers (i.e., a given ideological score in one chamber meant the same thing as that score in the other chamber), they were dubbed common space scores. Poole's extension derives scores for all presidents since President Dwight Eisenhower that are comparable to those for senators and members of the House of Representatives.

7. The Giles, Hettinger, and Peppers scores apply to courts of appeals judges. Since the model we ultimately test in this chapter also includes district court judges sitting by designation, we extend this measurement strategy to district court judges as well.

8. 28 U.S.C. § 332(d).

9. We identified chief judges and their dates of service from the Federal Judicial Center's Web site (http://www.fjc.gov).

10. There is a great deal of research regarding the acclimation of justices to the U.S. Supreme Court, in terms of both voting behavior (e.g., Snyder 1958; Hagle 1993) and opinion authorship (e.g., Bowen 1995; Bowen and Scheb 1993; Brenner and Hagle 1996). In contrast, there is very little scholarship regarding the existence of a freshman effect on other courts. The few exceptions include work by Carp and Wheeler (1972) on federal district court judges and work by Howard (1981) and Wasby (1989) on courts of appeals judges.

11. We determined each judge's freshman period based on information available in Zuk, Barrow, and Gryski (1997). We identified each judge's appointment from this source and calculated whether the decision in each case occurred within two years of that date.

12. Similar to our identification of freshman judges, we used information available from Zuk, Barrow, and Gryski (1997) to identify senior judges.

13. We relied on the coding criteria in the Songer Database, which clearly distinguishes district court judges sitting by designation.

14. Both prior federal and prior appellate court experience was ascertained based on information contained in Zuk, Barrow, and Gryski (1997).

15. Sheldon Goldman kindly provided the information on ABA scores for each judge.

16. Data on amicus curiae participation are available in the Songer Database.

17. Data on civil rights and civil liberties claims are available in the Songer Database.

18. Measuring the presence of cross appeals is a straightforward matter. Cross appeals are either present or absent in a given case, and this information is readily available in the Songer Database. Measuring the number of legal issues raised is a more difficult task. The Songer Database contains a set of variables that reflects the number of different references in the headnotes set forth at the beginning of the majority opinion in West's *Federal Reporter*. Combined, this set of variables offers a reasonable approximation of the total number of issues raised.

19. Data on circuit court reversal of a district court are available in the Songer Database.

20. To do this, we gathered information from Westlaw regarding the percentage of published decisions with separate opinions, which we lagged one year.

21. This measure is based on information available from the Federal Judicial Center on their Web site (http://www.fjc.gov).

22. Of course, this might not be true depending on the nature of those heavier workloads. If one circuit has a higher workload in terms of the number of the cases on its docket but those cases, on average, are "easier" than those of a circuit with fewer cases on its docket, workload in terms of the amount of time it takes to process their respective caseloads may be equivalent.

23. The measure we employ reflects the number of merits terminations per judge by circuit and year, as recorded by the Administrative Office of the U.S. Courts in its annual reports.

24. Note that these figures are lower than the percentage of cases with dissents or concurrences, because each case can have two observations (rather than the single observation at the case level).

25. The MNL model is a form of discrete choice model "based on the principle that an individual chooses the outcome that maximizes the utility gained from that choice"

(Long 1997, 155). We describe this technique in a methodological appendix at the end of this book.

26. There are other statistical tools that are appropriate for analyzing discrete choices. The MNL model, however, is the most appropriate in the present circumstances. In general, MNL assumes the "independence of irrelevant alternatives" (IIA) in that the choice "can plausibly be assumed to be distinct and weighted independently" (Long 1997, 183). If this assumption is not met, the results of the statistical estimation are suspect. To ensure that this assumption was appropriate in our case, we conducted a Hausman test for the IIA property and found that the IIA assumption was not violated (see Long 1997, 183).

FOUR The Strategy of Dissent

1. Arguably, however, Schubert beat Murphy to the punch with his 1958 article on the decision making of New Deal Supreme Court justices.

2. Two contemporary champions of the strategic model suggest that the reason for this is that Murphy's work was chock full of rich intuitions but lacked systematic evidence to support them (Epstein and Knight 1998, xi–xii).

3. Subsequent work on state judicial review further elaborates on the conditioning effect of state judicial selection mechanisms (Brace, Hall, and Langer 1997; Langer 2002).

4. The work by Tanenhaus and his colleagues (Tanenhaus, Schick, Muraskin, and Rosen 1963) is considered a classic in this area (see, also, Teger and Kosinski 1980). Perry's (1991) more recent work is also an important contribution.

5. As Van Winkle himself noted, his results, based on a single issue area and a single year, may not be representative of dissenting behavior on the courts of appeals more generally (1997, 17–18).

6. Note that the lack of an effect for strategic considerations holds true even when we limit analysis to those cases judges arguably care most about and hence might be willing to expend the necessary resources to engage in strategic calculations (those involving civil rights or civil liberties claims).

FIVE The Decision to Reverse

1. See table 5.1 in Songer, Sheehan, and Haire (2000).

2. Table B-5, Administrative Office of the U.S. Courts, *Judicial Business of the United States Courts: Annual Report of the Director,* (2003).

3. Circuit judicial councils operate as the governing bodies for the individual. The Judicial Conference of the United States is the chief policymaking body of the federal courts.

4. We used the ideology of the majority opinion writer for purposes of consistency with our analyses in chapters 3 and 4, but note that our substantive results were essentially identical to those obtained when using the average ideological score for all panel members.

5. We identified chief judges and their dates of service based on information available from the Federal Judicial Center's Web site (http://www.fjc.gov) and ascertained the freshman status of judges based on information available in Zuk, Barrow, and Gryski (1997).

6. Information on both the presence of civil rights/civil liberties claims and the presence of amicus curiae is available in the Songer Database.

7. Arguably, appellate judges reviewing a complex case may also be more prone to reverse because such legal complexity requires more care and effort in the process of review. This enhanced scrutiny could result in more-frequent identification of reversible error. To the extent that this is true, then complexity in a case might lead more frequently to reversal, because (a) the district court judge is more likely to make a reversible error and (b) the courts of appeals panel is more likely to catch reversible error.

8. Information on both of these variables is available in the Songer Database.

9. See table 5.1 in Songer, Sheehan, and Haire (2000). These data pertain to cases decided with published opinion. The dissent rate is considerably lower if cases with unpublished opinions are included in the denominator.

10. Dissent rates by circuit and year were calculated based on information available in the Songer Database.

11. Information on circuit size is available from the Web site of the Federal Judicial Center (http://www.fjc.gov).

12. The measure we employ reflects the number of merits terminations per judge by circuit and year, as recorded by the Administrative Office of the U.S. Courts in its annual reports.

13. Reversal rates by circuit and year were calculated based on information available in the Songer Database.

14. In some instances, the formal ruling is to affirm the lower court ruling. Alternatively, a circuit court panel can simply dismiss an appeal, which is functionally equivalent to affirming the district court ruling.

15. Other functional equivalents include reverse and vacate, remand, set aside and remand, as well as modify and remand.

16. In this baseline analysis then, we assume that the three-judge panel has neither a chief judge nor a district court judge as one of its three members. The baseline probability is also based on the assumption that the case does not involve an amicus curiae brief, a civil liberties issue, or a cross appeal. Further, the baseline probability assumes the appellant's counsel is paid or experienced.

Conclusions

1. This percentage is based only on cases with published opinions; the overall separate opinion rate is much lower when all cases are considered.

2. As Peltason has observed, "[T]he decision as to who will make the decisions affects what decisions will be made" (1955: 29).

3. There is a rich literature devoted to the specification of judges' goals (or utility functions, in the parlance of economic analysis). See Baum (1997) for a thorough overview.

4. Of course, some critical legal theorists might argue that most rules are sufficiently indeterminate to justify alternative outcomes and the fact that some legal issues appear "settled" is simply a matter of prevailing social conditions that fail (currently) to promote challenges to the particular rule (see Tushnet 1996).

Administrative Office of the United States Courts. 2002, 2003. *Judicial Business of the United States Courts: Annual Report of the Director.* Washington, DC: U.S. Government Printing Office.

Alexander, A. Lamar, Jr. 1965. "En Banc Hearings in the Federal Courts of Appeals: Institutional Responsibilities." *New York University Law Review* 40:562–608.

Allison, Garland W. 1996. "Delay in Senate Confirmation of Federal Judicial Nominees." *Judicature* 80:8–15.

American Bar Association. 1994. *Standards Relating to Appellate Courts.* Chicago: American Bar Association.

Atkins, Burton M. 1973. "Judicial Behavior and Tendencies toward Conformity in a Three Member Small Group: A Case Study of Dissent Behavior on the U.S. Courts of Appeals." *Social Science Quarterly* 54:41–53.

———. 1990. "Interventions and Power in Judicial Hierarchies: Appellate Courts in England and the United States." *Law and Society Review* 24:71–105.

Atkins, Burton M., and Justin J. Green. 1976. "Consensus on the United States Courts of Appeals: Illusion or Reality?" *American Journal of Political Science* 20:735–48.

Atkins, Burton M., and William Zavoina. 1974. "Judicial Leadership on the Court of Appeals: A Probability Analysis of Panel Assignment in Race Relations Cases on the Fifth Circuit." *American Journal of Political Science* 18:701–11.

Baker, Thomas E. 1994. *Rationing Justice on Appeal: The Problems of the U.S. Courts of Appeals.* St. Paul: West Publishing.

Barker, Lucius. 1967. "Third Parties in Litigation: A Systematic View of the Judicial Function." *Journal of Politics* 29:41–69.

Bass, Jack. 1981. *Unlikely Heroes: The Dramatic Story of the Southern Judges of the Fifth Circuit Who Translated the Supreme Court's Brown Decision into a Revolution for Equality.* New York: Simon and Schuster.

Baum, Lawrence. 1980. "Responses of Federal District Judges to Court of Appeals Policies: An Exploration." *Western Political Quarterly* 33:217–24.

———. 1997. *The Puzzle of Judicial Behavior.* Ann Arbor: University of Michigan Press.

Bell, Lauren Cohen. 2002a. "Senatorial Discourtesy: The Senate's Use of Delay to Shape the Federal Judiciary." *Political Research Quarterly* 55:589–607.

———. 2002b. *Warring Factions: Interest Groups, Money and the New Politics of Senate Confirmation.* Columbus: Ohio State University Press.

Benesh, Sara C. 2002. *The U.S. Court of Appeals and the Law of Confessions: Perspectives on the Hierarchy of Justice.* New York: LFB Scholarly Publishing.

Binder, Sarah A., and Forrest Maltzman. 2002. "Senatorial Delay in Confirming Judges, 1947–1998." *American Journal of Political Science* 46:190–99.

Boucher, Robert L., Jr., and Jeffrey A. Segal. 1995. "Supreme Court Justices as Strategic Decision Makers: Aggressive Grants and Defensive Denials on the Vinson Court." *Journal of Politics* 57:824–37.

Bowen, Terry. 1995. "Consensual Norms and the Freshman Effect on the United States Supreme Court." *Social Science Quarterly* 76:222–31.

Bowen, Terry, and John M. Scheb II. 1993. "Freshman Opinion Writing on the U.S. Supreme Court, 1921–1991." *Judicature* 76:239–43.

Brace, Paul, and Melinda Gann Hall. 1990. "Neo-Institutionalism and Dissent in State Supreme Courts." *Journal of Politics* 52:54–70.

———. 1993. "Integrated Models of Dissent." *Journal of Politics* 55:914–35.

Brace, Paul, Melinda Gann Hall, and Laura Langer. 1997. "Judicial Review of Legislation: Implications for Judicial Independence and the Autonomy of Courts." Paper presented at the World Congress of the International Political Science Association. Seoul, Korea.

Brennan, William. 1986. "In Defense of Dissents." *Hastings Law Journal* 37:427–38.

Brenner, Saul, and Timothy M. Hagle. 1996. "Opinion Writing and Acclimation Effect." *Political Behavior* 18:235–61.

Brenner, Saul, and John F. Krol. 1989. "Strategies in Certiorari Voting on the United States Supreme Court." *Journal of Politics* 51:828–40.

Brenner, Saul, and Harold J. Spaeth. 1988. "Majority Opinion Assignments and the Maintenance of the Original Coalition on the Warren Court." *American Journal of Political Science* 32:72–81.

Brudney, James J., and Corey Ditslear. 2001. "Designated Diffidence: District Court Judges on the Courts of Appeals." *Law and Society Review* 35:565–606.

Bureau of Justice Statistics. 1993. *State Court Organization.* Williamsburg, VA: National Center for State Courts.

Caldeira, Gregory A., John R. Wright, and Christopher J. W. Zorn. 1999. "Sophisticated Voting and Gate-Keeping in the Supreme Court." *Journal of Law, Economics, and Organization* 15:549–72.

Cameron, Charles M., Jeffrey A. Segal, and Donald Songer. 2000. "Strategic Auditing in a Political Hierarchy: An Informational Model of the Supreme Court's Certiorari Decision." *American Political Science Review* 94:101–16.

Caminker, Evan H. 1994. "Why Must Inferior Courts Obey Superior Court Precedents?" *Stanford Law Review* 46:817–73.

Canon, Bradley C. 1973. "Reactions of State Supreme Courts to a U.S. Supreme Court Civil Liberties Decision." *Law and Society Review* 8:109–34.

———. 1974. "Is the Exclusionary Rule in Failing Health? Some New Data and a Plea against Precipitous Conclusions." *Kentucky Law Journal* 62:681–730.

Carp, Robert A., and C. K. Rowland. 1983. *Policymaking and Politics in the Federal District Courts.* Knoxville: University of Tennessee Press.

Carp, Robert A., and Ronald Stidham. 1998. *The Federal Courts,* 3rd ed. Washington, DC: CQ Press.

Carp, Robert A., Ronald Stidham, and Kenneth L. Manning. 2004. *Judicial Process in America,* 6th ed. Washington, DC: Congressional Quarterly Press.

Carp, Robert A., and Russell Wheeler. 1972. "Sink or Swim: The Socialization of a Federal District Judge." *Journal of Public Law* 21:359–92.

Carrington, Paul. 1969. "Crowded Dockets and the Courts of Appeals: The Threat to the Function of Review and the National Law." *Harvard Law Review* 82:542–617.

Chase, Harold. 1972. *Federal Judges: The Appointing Process.* Minneapolis: University of Minnesota Press.

Citizens for Independent Courts. 2000. *Uncertain Justice: Politics and America's Courts.* New York: Century Foundation Press.

Coffin, Frank. 1994. *On Appeal: Courts, Lawyering and Judging.* New York: W. W. Norton.

Cohen, Jonathan Matthew. 2002. *Inside Appellate Courts: The Impact of Court Organization on Judicial Decision Making in the United States Courts of Appeals.* Ann Arbor: University of Michigan Press.

Cole, Kenneth. 1937. "Mr. Justice Black and 'Senatorial Courtesy.'" *American Political Science Review* 31:1113–15.

Collins, Paul M., Jr. 2004. "Friends of the Court: Examining the Influence of Amicus Curiae Participation in U.S. Supreme Court Litigation." *Law and Society Review.* 38:807–32.

Cross, Frank, and Emerson Tiller. 1998. "Judicial Partisanship and Obedience to Legal Doctrine: Whistleblowing on the Federal Courts of Appeals." *Yale Law Journal* 107:2155–76.

Dawson, Richard E., Kenneth Prewitt, and Karen Dawson. 1977. *Political Socialization,* 2nd ed. Glenview, IL: Scott, Foresman and Company.

Drahozal, Christopher R. 1998. "Judicial Incentives and the Appeals Process." *Southern Methodist Law Review* 51:469–503.

Duxbury, Neil. 1995. *Patterns of American Jurisprudence.* Oxford, NY: Oxford University Press.

Easton, David. 1953. *The Political System.* New York: Knopf.

Easton, David, and Jack Dennis. 1969. *Children in the Political System: Origins of Political Legitimacy.* New York: McGraw Hill.

Edwards, Harry T. 1991. "The Judicial Function and the Elusive Goal of Principled Decisionmaking." *Wisconsin Law Review* September/October: 837–65.

Epp, Charles R. 1990. "Connecting Litigation Levels and Legal Mobilization: Explaining Interstate Variation in Employment Civil Rights Litigation." *Law and Society Review* 24:145–61.

Epstein, Lee. 1991. "Courts and Interest Groups." In *The American Courts: A Critical Assessment,* eds. John B. Gates and Charles A. Johnson. Washington, DC: CQ Press.

Epstein, Lee, and Jack Knight. 1998. *The Choices Justices Make.* Washington, DC: CQ Press.

Epstein, Lee, Jeffrey A. Segal, Harold J. Spaeth, and Thomas G. Walker. 2003. *Supreme Court Compendium,* 3rd ed. Washington, DC: CQ Press.

Eskridge, William. 1991. "Overriding Supreme Court Statutory Interpretation Decisions." *Yale Law Journal* 101:331–425.

Feinberg, Wilfred. 1984. "The Office of Chief Judge of a Federal Court of Appeals." *Fordham Law Review* 53:369–89.

———. 1990. "Senior Judges: A National Resource." *Brooklyn Law Review* 56:409–18.

Firestone, David. 2003. "Washington: Senate Backs 'Under God.'" *New York Times,* 5 March.

Fisher, Gregory S. 2003. "The Greatest Dissent? A Brief Essay on Language, Law, Rule and Reason." *Federal Lawyer* 50:30–34.

Flanders, Robert G., Jr. 1999. "The Utility of Separate Judicial Opinions in Appellate Courts of Last Resort: Why Dissents Are Valuable." *Roger Williams University Law Review* 4:401–24.

Foskett, Ken. 2002. "Bush, Congress Blast Ruling against Pledge." *Atlanta Journal-Constitution,* 28 June.

Frankfurter, Felix, and James M. Landis. 1927. *The Business of the Supreme Court: A Study in the Federal Judicial System.* New York: MacMillan Company.

Freeman, Michael D. A. 1994. *Lloyd's Introduction to Jurisprudence,* 6th ed. London: Sweet and Maxwell Ltd.

Friendly, Henry J. 1961. "Book Review: The Common Law Tradition—Deciding Appeals." *University of Pennsylvania Law Review* 109:1040–45.

———. 1982. "Indiscretion about Discretion." *Emory Law Journal* 31:747–84.

Garbus, Marvin. 2003. *Courting Disaster: The Supreme Court and the Unmaking of American Law.* New York: Henry Holt and Company.

Gely, Rafael, and Pablo T. Spiller. 1990. "A Rational Choice Theory of Supreme Court Statutory Decisions with Applications to the *State Farm* and *Grove City Cases.*" *Journal of Law, Economics and Organization* 6:263–300.

———. 1992. "The Political Economy of Supreme Court Constitutional Decisions: The Case of Roosevelt's Court-Packing Plan." *International Review of Law and Economics* 12:45–67.

George, Tracey E. 1999. "The Dynamics and Determinants of the Decision to Grant En Banc Review." *Washington Law Review* 74:213–74.

George, Tracey E., and Reginald S. Sheehan. 2000. "Circuit Breaker: Deciphering Courts of Appeals Decisions Using the U.S. Courts of Appeals Data Base." *Judicature* 83:240–47.

George, Tracey E., and Michael E. Solimine. 2001. "Supreme Court Monitoring of the United States Courts of Appeals En Banc." *Supreme Court Economic Review* 9:171–204.

Gerhart, Eugene C. 1958. *America's Advocate: Robert H. Jackson.* Indianapolis: Bobbs-Merrill.

Giles, Micheal W., Virginia A. Hettinger, and Todd Peppers. 2001. "Picking Federal Judges: A Note on Policy and Partisan Selection Agendas." *Political Research Quarterly* 54:623–41.

———. 2002. "Measuring the Preferences of Federal Judges: Alternatives to Party of the Appointing President." Emory University. Typescript.

Ginsburg, Douglas H., and Donald Falk. 1991. "The Court En Banc: 1981–1990." *George Washington Law Review* 59:1008–53.

Glick, Henry R., and George W. Pruet Jr. 1986. "Dissent in State Supreme Courts: Patterns and Correlates of Conflict." In *Judicial Conflict and Consensus: Behavioral Studies of American Appellate Courts,* eds. Sheldon Goldman and Charles M. Lamb. Lexington: University Press of Kentucky.

Goldman, Sheldon. 1966. "Voting Behavior on the United States Courts of Appeals, 1961–1964." *American Political Science Review* 60:374–83.

———. 1967. "Judicial Appointments to the United States Courts of Appeals." *Wisconsin Law Review* 86:186–214.

———. 1969. "Backgrounds, Attitudes, and the Voting Behavior of Judges: A Comment on Joel Grossman's Social Backgrounds and Judicial Decisions." *Journal of Politics* 31:214–22.

———. 1975. "Voting Behavior on the U.S. Courts of Appeals Revisited." *American Political Science Review* 69:491–506.

———. 1997. *Picking Federal Judges.* New Haven, CT: Yale University Press.

Goldman, Sheldon, and Charles M. Lamb. 1986. "Prologue." In *Judicial Conflict and Consensus: Behavioral Studies of American Appellate Courts,* eds. Sheldon Goldman and Charles M. Lamb. Lexington: University Press of Kentucky.

Green, Donald R. 1986. "Parameters of Dissensus on Shifting Small Groups." In *Judicial Conflict and Consensus: Behavioral Studies of American Appellate Courts,* eds. Sheldon Goldman and Charles M. Lamb. Lexington: University Press of Kentucky.

Green, Justin J., and Burton M. Atkins. 1978. "Designated Judges: How Well Do They Perform?" *Judicature* 6:358–70.

Groner, Jonathan. 1996. "As Judge-Picker, Dole Is No Ronald Reagan." *Legal Times,* 1 April.

Grossman, Joel B. 1964. "Federal Judicial Selection: The Work of the ABA Committee." *Midwest Journal of Political Science* 8:221–54.

Gruhl, John. 1980. "The Supreme Court's Impact on the Law of Libel: Compliance by Lower Federal Courts." *Western Political Quarterly* 33:502–19.

Hagle, Timothy M. 1993. "'Freshman Effects' for Supreme Court Justices." *American Journal of Political Science* 37:1142–57.

Haire, Susan B., Stefanie A. Lindquist, and Roger Hartley. 1999. "Attorney Expertise, Litigant Success, and Judicial Decisionmaking in the U.S. Courts of Appeals." *Law and Society Review* 33:667–86.

Haire, Susan B., Stefanie A. Lindquist, and Donald R. Songer. 2003. "Appellate Court Supervision in the Federal Judiciary: A Hierarchical Perspective." *Law and Society Review* 37:143–68.

Hall, Melinda Gann. 1992. "Electoral Politics and Strategic Voting in State Supreme Courts." *Journal of Politics* 54:427–46.

———. 1995. "Justices as Representatives: Elections and Judicial Politics in the American States." *American Politics Quarterly* 23:485–503.

Hall, Melinda Gann, and Paul Brace. 1989. "Order in the Courts: A Neo-Institutional Approach to Judicial Consensus." *Western Political Quarterly* 42:391–407.

———. 1992. "Toward an Integrated Model of Judicial Voting Behavior." *American Politics Quarterly* 20:147–68.

———. 1999. "State Supreme Courts and Their Environments: Avenues to General Theories of Judicial Choice." In *Supreme Court Decision-Making: New Institutionalist Approaches,* eds. Cornell W. Clayton and Howard Gillman. Chicago: University of Chicago Press.

Hand, Learned. 1958. *The Bill of Rights.* Cambridge, MA: Harvard University Press.

Hanssen, F. Andrew. 1999. "The Effect of Judicial Institutions on Uncertainty and the Rate of Litigation: The Election Versus Appointment of State Judges." *Journal of Legal Studies* 28:205–32.

Hartley, Roger E., and Lisa Holmes. 1997. "Increasing Senate Scrutiny of Lower Federal Court Nominees." *Judicature* 80:274–78.

———. 2002. "The Increasing Senate Scrutiny of Lower Federal Court Nominees." *Political Science Quarterly* 117:259–78.

Haynie, Stacia L. 1992. "Leadership and Consensus on the U.S. Supreme Court." *Journal of Politics* 54:1158–69.

Heck, Edward V., and Melinda Gann Hall. 1981. "Bloc Voting and the Freshman Justice Revisited." *Journal of Politics* 43:852–60.

Hellman, Arthur D. 1999. "Precedent, Predictability, and Federal Appellate Structure." *University of Pittsburgh Law Review* 60:1029–1109.

———. 2000. "Getting It Right: Panel Error and the En Banc Process in the Ninth Circuit Court of Appeals." *University of California-Davis Law Review* 34:425–69.

Hettinger, Virginia A. 1999. "The Supreme Court as an Independent Policy Maker: Statutory Interpretation and the Separation of Powers." Ph.D. dissertation, Emory University.

Hettinger, Virginia A., Stefanie A. Lindquist, and Wendy L. Martinek. 2003a. "Acclimation Effects on the United States Courts of Appeals." *Social Science Quarterly* 84:792–810.

———. 2003b. "The Role and Impact of Chief Judges on the United States Courts of Appeals." *Justice System Journal* 24:91–117.

———. 2003c. "Separate Opinion Writing on the United States Courts of Appeals." *American Politics Research* 31:215–50.

———. 2004. "Comparing Attitudinal and Strategic Accounts of Dissenting Behavior on the U.S. Courts of Appeals." *American Journal of Political Science* 48:123–37.

Higgins, Richard S., and Paul H. Rubin. 1980. "Judicial Discretion." *Journal of Legal Studies* 9:129–38.

Holmes, Oliver Wendell, Jr. 1897. "The Path of the Law." *Harvard Law Review* 10:457–78.

Hood, M. V., III, Quentin Kidd, and Irwin L. Morris. 1999. "Of Byrd[s] and Bumpers: Using Democratic Senators to Analyze Political Change in the South, 1960–1995." *American Journal of Political Science* 43:465–87.

Horowitz, Donald. 1977. *The Courts and Social Policy.* Washington, DC: Brookings.

Howard, J. Woodford. 1981. *Courts of Appeals in the Federal Judicial System: A Study of the Second, Fifth, and District of Columbia Circuits.* Princeton, NJ: Princeton University Press.

Hutchinson, Allan C. 1989. "Democracy and Determinacy: An Essay on Legal Interpretation." *University of Miami Law Review* 43:541–76.

"Judges: Attacks on Baer Go Too Far." 1996. *Legal Times*, 1 April.

Kadzielski, Mark A., and Robert C. Kunda. 1983. "The Origins of Modern Dissent: The Unmaking of Judicial Consensus in the 1930s." *University of Washington Law Review* 15:43–76.

Kirkpatrick, Samuel A., and Lelan McLemore. 1977. "Perceptual and Affective Components of Legislative Norms: A Social-Psychological Analysis of Congruity." *Journal of Politics* 39:685–711.

Klein, David E. 2002. *Making Law in the United States Courts of Appeals.* New York: Cambridge University Press.

Klein, David E., and Robert J. Hume. 2003. "Fear of Reversal as an Explanation for Lower Court Compliance." *Law and Society Review* 37:579–606.

Klein, David, and Darby Morrisroe. 1999. "The Prestige and Influence of Individual Judges on the U.S. Courts of Appeals." *Journal of Legal Studies* 28:371–91.

Kornhauser, Lewis A. 1995. "Adjudication by a Resource-Constrained Team: Hierarchy and Precedent in a Judicial System." *Southern California Law Review* 68:1605–29.

———. 1999. "Appeal and Supreme Courts." In *Encyclopedia of Law and Economics.* http://encyclo.findlaw.com/7200book.pdf, accessed July 13, 2004.

Kornhauser, Lewis A., and Lawrence G. Sager. 1989. "Unpacking the Court." *Yale Law Journal* 96:82–117.

Kozinski, Alex. 1993. "What I Ate for Breakfast and Other Mysteries of Judicial Decision Making." *Loyola of Los Angeles Law Review* 26:993–99.

Kozlowski, Mark. 2003. *The Myth of the Imperial Judiciary: Why the Right Is Wrong about the Courts.* New York: New York University Press.

Krehbiel, Keith. 1992. *Information and Legislative Organization.* Ann Arbor: University of Michigan Press.

Kritzer, Herbert M., and Mark J. Richards. 2003. "Jurisprudential Regimes and Supreme Court Decisionmaking: The *Lemon* Regime and Establishment Clause Cases." *Law and Society Review* 37:827–40.

Kuersten, Ashlyn, and Donald R. Songer. 2001. *Decisions on the U.S. Courts of Appeals.* New York: Garland Publishing.

Lamb, Charles M. 1986. "A Microlevel Analysis of Appeals Court Conflict: Warren Burger and His Colleagues on the DC Circuit." In *Judicial Conflict and Consensus: Behavioral Studies of American Appellate Courts,* eds. Sheldon Goldman and Charles M. Lamb. Lexington: University of Kentucky Press.

Landes, William M., and Richard A. Posner. 1979. "Adjudication as a Public Good." *Journal of Legal Studies* 8:235–84.

Langer, Laura. 1997. "State Supreme Courts and Countermajoritarian Behavior: Strategic or Sincere?" Paper presented at the Conference on the Scientific Study of Judicial Politics. Atlanta, Georgia: Emory University.

———. 1999. "Strategic Behavior and Policy Saliency to the Elected Elites: A Comparative Examination of State Judicial Review across Four Areas of Law 1970–1993." Paper presented at the Annual Meeting of the Midwest Political Science Association. Chicago, Illinois.

———. 2002. *Judicial Review in State Supreme Courts: A Comparative Study.* Albany: State University of New York Press.

Long, J. Scott. 1997. *Regression Models for Categorical and Limited Dependent Variables.* Thousand Oaks, CA: Sage.

Lumbard, J. Edward. 1968. "Current Problems of the Federal Courts of Appeals." *Cornell Law Review* 54:29–44.

Macey, Jonathan R. 1997. "The Internal and External Costs and Benefits of Stare Decisis." In *Public Choice and Public Law: Readings and Commentary,* ed. Maxwell L. Stearns. Cincinnati, OH: Anderson Publishing Co.

Maltzman, Forrest, James F. Spriggs II, and Paul J. Wahlbeck. 2000. *Crafting Law on the Supreme Court: The Collegial Game.* New York: Cambridge University Press.

March, James G., and Johan P. Olsen. 1984. "The New Institutionalism: Organizational Factors in Political Life." *American Political Science Review* 78:734–49.

Martinek, Wendy L., Mark Kemper, and Steven R. Van Winkle. 2002. "To Advise and Consent: The Senate and Lower Federal Court Nominations, 1977–1998." *Journal of Politics* 64:337–61.

Massie, Tajuana, Thomas G. Hansford, and Donald R. Songer. 2004. "The Timing of Presidential Nominations to the Lower Federal Courts." *Political Research Quarterly* 57:145–54.

Mather, Lynn. 1995. "The Fired Football Coach (Or, How Trial Courts Make Policy)." In *Contemplating Courts,* ed. Lee Epstein. Washington, DC: Congressional Quarterly Press.

Miceli, Thomas J., and Metin M. Coşgel. 1994. "Reputation and Judicial Decision-Making." *Journal of Economic Behavior and Organization* 23:31–51.

Murphy, Walter F. 1959. "Lower Court Checks on Supreme Court Power." *American Political Science Review* 53:1017–31.

———. 1964. *Elements of Judicial Strategy.* Chicago: University of Chicago Press.

———. 1966. "Courts as Small Groups." *Harvard Law Review* 79:1565–72.

National Center for State Courts. 1997. *Caseload Statistics: Examining the Work of the State Courts.* Williamsburg, VA: National Center for State Courts.

Neely, Richard. 1981. *How Courts Govern America.* New Haven, CT: Yale University Press.

Newman, Jon O. 1984. "Between Legal Realism and Neutral Principles: The Legitimacy of Institutional Values." *California Law Review* 72:200–216.

———. 1992. "A Study of Appellate Reversals." *Brooklyn Law Review* 58:629–40.

———. 1993. "1,000 Judges—The Limit for an Effective Judiciary." *Judicature* 76:187–88, 194.

Niemi, Richard G., and Barbara J. Sobieszek. 1977. "Political Socialization." *Annual Review of Sociology* 3:209–33.

Nixon, David C., and David L. Goss. 2001. "Confirmation Delay for Vacancies on the Circuit Courts of Appeals." *American Politics Research* 29:246–74.

O'Connor, Francis P. 1998. "The Art of Collegiality: Creating Consensus and Coping with Dissent." *Massachusetts Law Review* 83:93–96.

Pacelle, Richard, and Patricia Pauly. 1996. "The Freshman Effect Revisited: An Individual-Based Analysis." *American Review of Politics* 17:1–22.

Patterson, John W., and Gregory J. Rathjen. 1976. "Background Diversity and State Supreme Court Dissent Behavior." *Polity* 8:610–22.

Peltason, Jack. 1955. *Federal Courts in the Political Process.* Garden City, NY: Doubleday.

———. 1961. *Fifty-Eight Lonely Men: Southern Federal Judges and School Desegregation.* New York: Harcourt Brace.

Peppers, Todd C., Katherine O'Harra-Vigilante, and Christopher Zorn. 2004. "Judicial Oversight and District Court Designation in the U.S. Courts of Appeals." Emory University. Typescript.

Perry, H. W., Jr. 1991. *Deciding to Decide: Agenda Setting in the United States Supreme Court.* Cambridge, MA: Harvard University Press.

Peterson, Steven A. 1981. "Dissent in American Courts." *Journal of Politics.* 43:412–34.

Polsby, Nelson W. 1968. "The Institutionalization of the U.S. House of Representatives." *American Political Science Review* 62:148–68.

Poole, Keith T. 1998. "Recovering a Basic Space from a Set of Issue Scales." *American Journal of Political Science* 42:954–93.

Poole, Keith T., and Howard Rosenthal. 1997. *Congress: A Political-Economic History of Roll Call Voting.* New York: Oxford University Press.

Posner, Richard A. 1985. *The Federal Courts: Crisis and Reform.* Cambridge, MA: Harvard University Press.

———. 1990. *The Problems of Jurisprudence.* Cambridge, MA: Harvard University Press.

———. 1995. *Overcoming Law.* Cambridge, MA: Harvard University Press.

———. 1997. "What Do Judges Maximize? The Same Thing that Everyone Else Does." In *Public Choice and Public Law: Readings and Commentary,* ed. Maxwell L. Stearns. Cincinnati: Anderson Publishing Co.

Powe, Lucas A., Jr. 2001. *The Warren Court and American Politics.* Cambridge, MA: Harvard University Press.

Priest, George L., and Benjamin Klein. 1984. "The Selection of Disputes for Litigation." *Journal of Legal Studies* 13:1–55.

Pritchett, C. Herman. 1941. "Divisions of Opinion among Justices of the U.S. Supreme Court." *American Political Science Review* 35:890–98.

———. 1948. *The Roosevelt Court: A Study in Judicial Politics and Values, 1937–1947.* New York: Macmillan Company.

———. 1954. *Civil Liberties and the Vinson Court.* Chicago: University of Chicago Press.

Rathjen, Gregory James. 1974. "Policy Goals, Strategic Choice, and Majority Opinion Assignments in the U.S. Supreme Court: A Replication." *American Journal of Political Science* 18:713–24.

Reddick, Anna Malia. 1997. The Applicability of Legal and Attitudinal Models to the Treatment of Precedent in the Courts of Appeals. Ph.D. dissertation, Michigan State University.

Reinhardt, Stephen. 1993. "Whose Federal Judiciary Is It Anyway?" *Loyola of Los Angeles Law Review* 27:1–7.

Rehnquist, William H. 1994. "1993 Year-End Report on the Federal Judiciary." *American Journal of Trial Advocacy* 17:571–80.

Richards, Mark J., and Herbert M. Kritzer. 2002. "Jurisprudential Regimes in Supreme Court Decision Making." *American Political Science Review* 96:305–20.

Richardson, Richard J., and Kenneth N. Vines. 1967. "Review, Dissent and the Appellate Process: A Political Interpretation." *Journal of Politics* 29:597–616.

———. 1970. *The Politics of Federal Courts: Lower Courts in the United States.* Boston: Little, Brown and Co.

Rohde, David. 1972. "Policy Goals, Strategic, Choice and Majority Opinion Assignments in the U.S. Supreme Court." *Midwest Journal of Political Science* 16:652–82.

Rohde, David, and Harold Spaeth. 1976. *Supreme Court Decision Making.* San Francisco: W. H. Freeman and Company.

Rosenberg, Gerald N. 1991. *The Hollow Hope: Can Courts Bring About Social Change?* Chicago: Chicago University Press.

Rowland, C. K. 1991. "The Federal District Courts." In *The American Courts: A Critical Assessment,* eds. John B. Gates and Charles A. Johnson. Washington, DC: CQ Press.

Rowland, C. K., and Robert A. Carp. 1996. *Politics and Judgment in Federal District Courts.* Lawrence: University of Kansas Press.

Russell, Thomas D. 2000. "The Shape of the Michigan River as Viewed from the Land of *Sweatt v. Painter* and *Hopwood.*" *Law and Social Inquiry* 25:507–20.

Salmon, Jacqueline L. 2003. "Scalia Defends Public Expression of Faith." *Washington Post,* 13 January.

Saphire, Richard B., and Michael E. Solimine. 1995. "Diluting Justice on Appeal?: An Examination of the Use of District Court Judges Sitting by Designation on the U.S. Courts of Appeals." *University of Michigan Journal of Law Reform* 28:351–407.

Scalia, Antonin. 1994. "The Dissenting Opinion." *Journal of Supreme Court History* 19:33–44.

Schubert, Glendon A. 1958. "The Study of Judicial Decision-Making as an Aspect of Political Behavior." *American Political Science Review* 52:1007–25.

———. 1962. "The 1960 Term of the Supreme Court: A Psychological Analysis." *American Political Science Review* 56:90–107.

———. 1965. *The Political Role of the Courts: Judicial Policy-Making.* Chicago: Scott, Foresman and Company.

Segal, Jeffrey A. 1997. "Separation-of-Powers Games in the Positive Theory of Congress and Courts." *American Political Science Review* 91:28–44.

Segal, Jeffrey A., and Harold J. Spaeth. 1993. *The Supreme Court and the Attitudinal Model.* New York: Cambridge University Press.

———. 2002. *The Supreme Court and the Attitudinal Model Revisited.* New York: Cambridge University Press.

Shavell, Steven. 1995. "The Appeals Process as a Means of Error Correction." *Journal of Legal Studies* 24:379–426.

Sheldon, Charles H. 1999. "The Incidence and Structure of Dissensus on a State Supreme Court." In *Supreme Court Decision Making: New Institutionalist Approaches,* eds. Cornell W. Clayton and Howard Gillman. Chicago: University of Chicago Press.

Sheldon, Charles H., and Linda A. Maule. 1997. *Choosing Justice: The Recruitment of State and Federal Judges.* Pullman: Washington State University Press.

Sickels, Robert J. 1965. "The Illusion of Judicial Consensus: Zoning Decisions in the Maryland Courts of Appeals." *American Political Science Review* 59:100–4.

Smith, Joseph L. 2004. "Patterns and Consequences of Judicial Reversals." Presented at the Annual Meeting of the Midwest Political Science Association, Chicago, Illinois.

Snyder, Eloise C. 1958. "The Supreme Court as a Small Group." *Social Forces* 36:232–38.

Solimine, Michael E. 1988. "Ideology and En Banc Review." *North Carolina Law Review* 67:29–76.

———. 1996. "The Three-Judge District Court in Voting Rights Litigation." *University of Michigan Journal of Law Reform* 30:79–145.

Songer, Donald R. 1982. "Consensual and Nonconsensual Decisions in Unanimous Opinions of the United States Courts of Appeals." *American Journal of Political Science* 26:225–39.

———. 1986. "Factors Affecting Variation in the Rates of Dissent in the U.S. Courts of Appeals." In *Judicial Conflict and Consensus,* eds. Sheldon Goldman and Charles M. Lamb. Lexington: University Press of Kentucky.

———. 1991. "The Circuit Courts of Appeals." In *The American Courts: A Critical Assessment,* eds. John B. Gates and Charles A. Johnson. Washington, DC: Congressional Quarterly Press.

———. 2002. *The United States Courts of Appeals Data Base.* Computer File. Ann Arbor: University of Michigan.

Songer, Donald R., and Sue Davis. 1990. "The Impact of Party and Region on Voting Decisions in the United States Courts of Appeals, 1955–1986." *Western Political Quarterly* 43:317–34.

Songer, Donald R., and Susan B. Haire. 1992. "Integrating Alternative Approaches to the Study of Judicial Voting: Obscenity Cases in the U.S. Courts of Appeals." *American Journal of Political Science* 36:963–82.

Songer, Donald R., Jeffrey A. Segal, and Charles M. Cameron. 1994. "The Hierarchy of Justice: Testing a Principal-Agent Model of Supreme Court-Circuit Court Interactions." *American Journal of Political Science* 38:673–96.

Songer, Donald R., and Reginald S. Sheehan. 1990. "Supreme Court Impact on Compliance and Outcomes: *Miranda* and *New York Times* in the United States Courts of Appeals." *Western Political Quarterly* 43:297–316.

Songer, Donald R., Reginald S. Sheehan, and Susan B. Haire. 2000. *Continuity and Change on the United States Courts of Appeals.* Ann Arbor: University of Michigan Press.

Spaeth, Harold, and Jeffrey Segal. 1999. *Majority Rule or Minority Will: Adherence to Precedent on the U.S. Supreme Court.* New York: Cambridge University Press.

Spiller, Pablo T., and Rafael Gely. 1992. "Congressional Control or Judicial Independence: The Determinants of U.S. Supreme Court Labor-Relations Decisions." *RAND Journal of Economics* 23:463–92.

Spitzer, Matt, and Eric Talley. 2000. "Judicial Auditing." *Journal of Legal Studies* 29:649–83.

Spriggs, James F., II. 2003. "The Attitudinal Model: An Explanation of Case Dispositions, Not Substantive Policy Outcomes." *Law and Courts* 13:23–26.

Strattmann, Thomas. 2000. "Congressional Voting over Legislative Careers: Shifting Positions and Changing Constraints." *American Political Science Review* 94:665–76.

Sunstein, Cass. 2003. *Why Societies Need Dissent.* Cambridge, MA: Harvard University Press.

Tanenhaus, Joseph, Marvin Schick, Matthew Muraskin, and Daniel Rosen. 1963. "The Supreme Court's Certiorari Jurisdiction: Cue Theory." In *Judicial Decision-Making,* ed. Glendon Schubert. New York: The Free Press.

Tate, Neal C., and Roger Handberg. 1991. "Time Binding and Theory Building in Personal Attribute Models of Supreme Court Voting Behavior, 1916–1988." *American Journal of Political Science* 35:460–80.

Teger, Stuart, and Douglas Kosinski. 1980. "The Cue Theory of Supreme Court Certiorari Jurisdiction: A Reconsideration." *Journal of Politics* 42:834–46.

Tushnet, Mark. 1996. "Defending the Indeterminacy Thesis." *Quinnipiac Law Review* 16:339–56.

Ulmer, S. Sidney. 1970. "Dissent Behavior and the Social Background of Supreme Court Justices." *Journal of Politics* 32:580–98.

———. 1971. *Courts as Small and Not So Small Groups.* New York: General Learning Press.

Van Duch, Darryl. 1996. "Senior Judge Ranks Close Vacancy Gap." *National Law Journal,* 22 July.

Van Natta, Don, Jr. 1996. "Judge Assailed over Drug Case Issues Reversal and an Apology." *New York Times,* 2 April.

Van Winkle, Steven R. 1997. "Dissent as a Signal: Evidence from the U.S. Courts of Appeals." Presented at the Annual Meeting of the American Political Science Association, Washington, DC.

Wahlbeck, Paul J., James F. Spriggs II, and Forrest Maltzman. 1999. "The Politics of Dissents and Concurrences on the U.S. Supreme Court." *American Politics Quarterly* 27:488–514.

Walker, Thomas G. 1973. "Behavioral Tendencies in the Three-Judge District Court." *American Journal of Political Science* 17:407–13.

———. 1997. "The Role of Norms in Institutional Evolution, Maintenance and Change." Presented at the Conference on the Scientific Study of Judicial Politics. Atlanta, Georgia: Emory University.

Wasby, Stephen L. 1980–81. "'Extra' Judges in a Federal Appellate Court: The Ninth Circuit." *Law and Society Review* 15:369–84.

———. 1989. "'Into the Soup?': The Acclimation of Ninth Circuit Appellate Judges." *Judicature* 73:10–16.

———. 2002. "How Do Courts of Appeals En Banc Decisions Fare in the U.S. Supreme Court." *Judicature* 85:182–89.

———. 2003. "The Work of a Circuit's Chief Judge." *Justice System Journal* 24: 63–90.

Watson, Tom. 1989. "Seniors Rescue Courts in Crisis." *Legal Times,* 19 June.

Wenner, Lettie McSpadden, and Lee E. Dutter. 1988. "Contextual Influence on Court Outcomes." *Western Political Quarterly* 41:115–34.

Wheeler, Russell R., and Charles W. Nihan. 1988. "Administering the Federal Judicial Circuits: A Survey of Chief Judges' Approaches and Procedures." In *Managing Appeals in Federal Courts,* eds. M. Tonry and R. A. Katzmann. Washington, DC: Federal Judicial Center.

Wood, Sandra L., Linda Camp Keith, Drew Noble Lanier, and Ayo Ogundele. 1998. "'Acclimation Effects' for Supreme Court Justices: A Cross-Validation, 1988–1940." *American Journal of Political Science* 42:690–97.

Zuk, Gary, Deborah J. Barrow, and Gerard S. Gryski. 1997. *A Multi-User Database on the Attributes of U.S. Appeals Court Judges.* Computer File. Ann Arbor, MI: Interuniversity Consortium for Political and Social Research.

INDEX

Constitutionalism
and Democracy